Fighting Forward

A Widow's Journey from Loss to Life

Jan Owen

To Tina —
Woman of Valor —
Keep fighting forward
with HOPE!

Jan Owen

Copyright

Author photography: Lauren Benson
Cover art: Shan Wallace, SDW Design
Editor: Lea Schafer

Published in the Unites States of America.

Contents

Dedication

I dedicate this book to you, my fellow widow warriors.
Always keep fighting forward.

In memory of Phil. You are forever loved.

Introduction

Becoming a widow at the age of forty-eight years old has opened my eyes to an entirely new world. I knew it existed, but was completely blind to the realities of widowhood. I believe I am not alone in this, a truth I now find a bit astounding. After all, in every single marriage, one partner will outlive the other. None of us live forever. Death and loss are realities we all will face. Widowhood is a common occurrence in life, yet it is rarely discussed and there are few resources or ministries devoted to those that are widowed. As I have walked this path, it almost seemed as if people, when widowed, became invisible, me included.

Everything changes for a woman, in particular, when she is widowed—her marital status, financial security, her social standing and even, many times, her support group. Oftentimes a woman has served as the primary caregiver (or only caregiver) for many years, and the stress of the death of her partner opens her to health risks.

On average, 75 percent of a widow's support base is lost, including a portion of family and friends, for various reasons.[1] Grief is complicated, and the death of a spouse touches every single area of a person's life, bringing with it secondary losses that increase the pain and suffering of the survivor. Women, specifically more than men, struggle to survive financially when widowed, and all will struggle to adjust and build a new life on their own.

The statistics are startling:

* In the United States alone, in 1998 there were 13,600,000 widowed persons.[2]

* Every year almost 800,000 women will lose their husbands and be widowed for an average of fourteen years.[3] **

* In the US 15 percent of widowed women will fall into poverty after being widowed. The Social Security Administration states, "...widowhood remains an important risk factor for transition into poverty. Faced with the loss of resources in widowhood, women have only a few options available to improve their economic status."[4] **

* There are 258,481,056 million widows worldwide, not including women who may have remarried. These women have 584,374,358 children.[5]

* A minimum of 38,261,345 widows worldwide live in extreme poverty, without their basic needs being met.[6] **

The statistics convinced me my personal experience was not unique. I was faced with becoming financially responsible for myself for the first time in my life after thirty years as a homemaker, caregiver and working in jobs with a lower salary or in the nonprofit sector. Like many women I had willingly sacrificed earning potential to care for my family. While I don't regret the choices I made, I am faced with challenges now because of them.

After being widowed, even though I had income, I still needed to find a career to support myself. In the midst of my grief I had to go back to school and learn new skills in order to build an entirely new life for myself. In light of all I have learned, I actually have a better situation than many. However, I still lacked the emotional support and empowerment that I needed to help me move forward.

Widows are a vital part of our population, yet their many needs go largely unnoticed and unaddressed. Each day I speak with widowed women in online forums. I see the pain they experience in grief, in financial difficulty, in the loss of emotional support from family and friends and in learning skills to function on their own. Widowhood is a tough road to travel, requiring those left behind to begin again under difficult circumstances, often the worst time of their lives. The journey requires courage and fortitude and a strength we didn't even know we possessed.

It is my hope that this book will be a hand of help and comfort to those who find themselves in the depths of grief after losing a spouse—or after any great loss—longing to begin again, daring to hope they are not alone as they fight forward. May it also shine a light on the plight of my fellow warrior widows and raise awareness of the needs of this community of people.

Part I:

This Is My Story

This Is My Story

Things happen in our life that take our breath away and completely break our heart. The pain feels unbearable, and we will know, if we were unsure before, that life is not fair. For me, the loss that brought me to my knees was the death of my husband of thirty years to a rare form of cancer just six days shy of his fiftieth birthday. Death changes everything. In particular, it changed me.

Before this tragedy, when I imagined how the loss of someone I love might affect me, I thought of the obvious—I would miss them, long for their company, feel without them. And this has been true. But loss is like a rock tossed into the middle of a placid pond: the waves go on and on, reaching far beyond the initial impact, touching places within my life I never foresaw or imagined. And it has left me forever altered. By this I don't mean an altered perspective, or finally becoming thankful for all of life, although that happened as well. I mean it changed me in ways that make it difficult for me to even recognize my own self.

When I glance back at the woman I was just four short years ago, she looks like a stranger to me. Now I seem like an older, wiser, more jaded woman with wild silver hair, a wrinkled, bare face and a deep knowing in her eyes looking back at a naive woman with perfect makeup and a fresh innocence who was still convinced that if we did all the right things in life, it would all turn out as we had dreamed. Oh, how wrong I was.

That realization, that full-frontal crash with reality has changed me from the inside out. I have a totally different perspective on life. I have faced the darkest places within myself and now know how easy it is to make mistakes, to choose a wrong path. I am at once more fragile than I was while also realizing just how strong I can be. I am more compassionate and less judgmental. I see life through new eyes. Grief has humbled me.

Sometimes the new knowledge is hard to bear. I long to go back many days, to a time when my life, in hindsight, seemed so very simple and—most of all—normal. Yet here I am, a new woman in many ways. And this is my story.

As you read, I don't want to give you the wrong impression. I loved my husband. However, we were suffering from some marital problems at the time of his diagnosis. He was diagnosed with severe depression, and I did not handle that well, even separating from him for a while. I ran from our problems; hiding from them and the anxiety I felt in dealing with them.

I admit freely that my greatest regret in life—one that I will live with forever—is wishing I had loved him better during our hard times. I often tell friends that Phil and I had twenty-six good years and four painful ones. So when you read the pages ahead, don't imagine me as some sort of superhero. See me as I really am: a woman who has loved mightily, failed terribly, fallen down, gotten back up and tried her hardest to walk the path in front of her anyway.

In the end Phil and I knew we loved each other. In fact the last words he uttered were to me on the day before he died. I woke up and went over to check on him, and I said, "Well, look who's awake! Good morning, sunshine!" Then I bent over and kissed his dry, chapped lips. He kissed me back awkwardly and said his last words. "I love you, too." In the end, that's all that mattered.

The Story

How do I even know where the story begins? The losses during that time of my life began a few years earlier—they affected me vocationally, they impacted my family and my marriage and they left me raw and hurting, wounded beyond belief.

Phil and I married young, two kids really, tying the knot when we were barely out of high school. Children quickly came along and we had three: a girl and two boys. We were a happy little family. It was almost like a fairy tale.

I was content to stay home with my babies when they were small. Phil finished his degree in engineering and went on to have a long career working for the government. His brilliance in math and with computers made him a natural for his job, and he enjoyed it. Our faith was important to us, and we often served together in church. Phil loved the students we worked with and was always willing to lend a hand if something needed building or fixing. He showed love most of all by doing what needed to be done.

Phil was my best friend. We loved to do things together, and one of those things we really enjoyed was traveling. We often explored new places and made many memories together in this way, taking the back roads, the dirt roads, longing to see what was around each new bend off the beaten path. Phil once said that we were best together when we were exploring the road less traveled. I think he was right.

As our children grew older, I began to work as a worship pastor in local churches. In 1998 I became the worship pastor at a church that was just starting. As a result, we moved to a different area of town and settled in, happy beyond belief. Phil oversaw the construction of the building; I led worship. We felt we were doing something that truly mattered. During that time, however, Phil suffered from severe depression. We told almost no one because he felt embarrassed, so it was a lonely time. Together we spent almost a year in counseling. I wondered if things would ever be the same. In truth, he continued to struggle on and off for the next fifteen years.

As time passed, our children left home and went off to college. We were sad but embraced the empty nest as a time to do things just for ourselves. Eventually, I left my position at church, a transition that was both difficult and painful. I started my own nonprofit and began to travel extensively to developing countries where I trained local church leaders. Phil's job demanded an extraordinary amount of travel from him as well. Right in the middle of all this, my mother began showing signs of dementia, and we knew we needed to move back home to be closer to her.

We built a beautiful new home on a bluff in the woods, right on the side of the mountain, close to both sets of parents. During our first few months after moving, in the midst of settling in, we received word that our eldest son, who had recently been diagnosed as having Bipolar Type II, had attempted suicide and was hospitalized. We loaded up the car and went to pick him up. In the end we brought him home to live with us to help keep him safe. This was one of my most difficult experiences as a parent to date.

Even though we both loved where we now lived, we began to experience a bit of emotional and physical exhaustion. We were closer to family, but farther from friends and our normal support network. I, in particular, felt isolated while at home. The work I did was intense, and it wore on me. And then, about ten months after we moved, Phil began to be depressed again. He hit bottom and could barely function. He would cry for hours, becoming clingy and even a bit obsessive, wanting me with him every second of the day. Our marriage suffered, and I began to experience severe anxiety.

In the end, I did not handle our marital issues well. The constant anxiety wore on me, and I asked for a separation, hiding out in a spare room that an elderly friend, a second mother figure, offered me. I forgot to eat; instead I slept, lost weight, and cried. Oh how I cried. It seemed the pain would not stop and I really thought things couldn't get worse, but I was so wrong.

One day during this time, while my husband, Phil, was away in a nearby city, I got a text that would change my life: "I urinated blood so I'm going to the ER. Maybe I have a kidney stone." I pushed it aside, telling myself it was surely nothing bad. A few hours later my phone rang.

"I have some bad news."

I could hear the terror in his voice. "What is it?"

"They did a CT scan and I have a tumor on my right kidney. I have kidney cancer."

I reeled in disbelief. That frozen, numbing cold climbed through my body and heart. My husband was healthy; he had never had a kidney stone or shown any signs of illness. It was hard to fathom what he'd been told.

It all seems like one big blur now, one long nightmare of doctor's visits, tests, surgery, more tests and always, always…more bad news. Many details remain unclear, forgotten in a haze of shock. Phil had his kidney removed, and we hoped that would be the cure. That was not the case.

When we went in for the test results, Dr. Hinson's voice echoed in the room. "Well, it looks like we got it all around the kidney, which is good news." He paused, taking a deep breath before going on. "Unfortunately, the pathology reports showed something surprising.

The surprise of my career, if I'm honest. You have a very rare, aggressive form of kidney cancer called collecting duct carcinoma. You'll need to go see an oncologist and have further tests to make sure it has not spread."

My mind and body were numb as we rode home in silence. After more tests we were told the cancer had spread to many places in his body, his bones and his lungs. I knew this meant stage IV, but we were told it was treatable. The oncologist insisted we go to University of Texas MD Anderson Cancer Center in Houston, Texas, where the foremost expert on this type of cancer practiced. After we checked in, they ushered us to an exam room.

It was totally white and sterile and cold. So cold. Phil kept taking my hand in his and rubbing it as if it were a lucky penny. We knew the doctors were looking at all the tests. In time an older physician with dark hair and a swarthy complexion came in. He tiredly sat down on the exam table, looking at Phil with great soberness.

"Well, it is definitely collecting duct cancer. I had hoped the path report was wrong because sometimes it is, but not this time." He cleared his throat, and Phil's grasp on my hand tightened. He looked straight at Phil and said in a matter-of-fact tone, "While we have options to help slow the growth of the cancer, there is no medical miracle available to you. If you're lucky, you might have two years."

Silence, then sobs. I couldn't tell if they were mine or Phil's. The world fell away. My head started spinning. I hung on to the edge of the chair, willing myself not to faint.

"So this is terminal?" Phil asked in a shaky voice.

"We don't use that word here."

"Well what do you call it then?"

"Incurable. We call it incurable," the doctor answered gruffly.

As if a different word made the nightmare not so.

I am sorry to say that my first thoughts at that moment were of myself. When I look back at this day, I am utterly ashamed of those feelings. They haunt me. I certainly felt horrible for Phil. I ached for our children, but this news left me reeling, wondering what I would do, how in the world I would handle this. Panic set in, as if the weight and responsibility for everyone had settled in one giant load sitting firmly on my shoulders. I feared I might buckle beneath it all.

We climbed into the car in shocked silence, not daring to meet one another's eyes. Something urged us to walk on the beach, where everything seems better. We drove to Galveston, riding in disbelief, the words we could not say lying heavy between us.

We parked at the edge of the sand and walked, hand in hand, people all around us, crossing our path, their lives unchanged, ours altered forever. Children played and ran, music blared, laughter punctuated the gentle roar of the surf. It felt surreal.

The sand was hard packed underneath our feet and felt so good. The sun was shining, and our steps flirted with the water's edge although the water was cool in March. I stopped and rolled up my pants' legs, and we even began to laugh a little. We walked and walked and let the ocean breeze blow against us as if that would blow away some of our heartache and pain.

Later we found a crowded seafood restaurant and sat at the bar, downing piña coladas and eating shrimp as if we had nothing more pressing to do. Haltingly we spoke of some things that must be done, such as checking insurance and telling our children and families. We ate golden bites of shrimp in between our tears. We knew that nothing could ever be the same.

The next day we flew home. Phil sat in the window seat, and I sat beside him. Exhausted, yet unable to sleep, we began to talk. I was almost afraid to say it, but finally I suggested, "Why don't you make a list of the things you want to do during this time?"

He pulled out a notebook and pen and bent over them, writing words I could not see. Occasionally he would stare out the window, clouds floating by as we flew, tears streaming down his face.

My heart started cracking open. My mind began to run through all the things he would miss, like seeing our children get married or holding our grandchildren. Africa. He had promised me for years that he'd go to Africa with me and we'd go on safari. Would we get to do that? I leaned my head over on his shoulder and whispered, "Can I see your list?"

Go back to Guatemala.
Go to the beach.
Go to Africa.
Dance with Maria.
Learn Spanish.

On and on it went, the last plans of a man who has been told his time is short.

"What would you put on it?" he asked me. "What do you want to do together?"

I sat and thought for a few moments. "I just want to be together. Spend time with the kids. It's really up to you."

Weeks passed, and the news never got any better. The cancer continued to march on, filling his body. He predictably lost his hair. He looked white and ghostly, the chemo and cancer both seeming to ravage his body. We did everything we could to prepare financially, physically. We put accounts in my name, paid off debt, friends helped around the house, and we did fun things on days he felt up to it. I entered counseling alone so that I could be brutally honest with at least one person about what I was feeling and how I was struggling.

In the coming month Phil condition worsened. The cancer spread rapidly. The doctor became concerned that Phil may have only a few months to live and shared that with me privately one day. It became obvious that we would not go back to Guatemala, we would not go to Disney World with the kids. It felt like another blow that I struggled to absorb.

That night after I put Phil to bed, I sat on the couch, exhausted by the day's news. I felt so tense, as if with the slightest touch I might crack wide open. Tears trickled down my cheeks, sobs shook my body. I began to cry noisily, the grief overtaking my body until I could no longer hold it back. I fell to the floor, wailing loudly, angrier than I had ever been in my life. I lay in the floor, and I began to kick and beat my hands against the carpet.

Screams of "Why?" were torn from somewhere deep inside me. This was not fair. We had always been good people. Why was this happening to us? I felt the enormity of it all wash over me, and finally I lay still, worn out from my tears.

We were given a gift in the fall as some new oral chemotherapy caused the cancer to stall. Nothing got better, but it did not grow for a while. We were able to make a few of those last dreams come true for our family. We traveled to New Orleans and strolled down Bourbon Street sipping hurricanes while laughing at the ridiculous sights we saw. We devoured beignets, stopped and watched street-corner musicians, walked on the levee in the cool of the day and absorbed the beauty, music and spirit of that city.

Phil and I visited Key West for the first time, where we ate our fill of shrimp and scallops and drank a Miami Vice or ten or twelve.

We bobbed in the gentle waves and took long, luxurious naps. Thanksgiving was spent in a cabin in the mountains, secluded yet all together. And we had one last Christmas together.

Things began to slide downhill in January, as if he had hung on and now was growing weary of the fight. We spent countless nights in the hospital, bones broken from cancer, pain overwhelming him. Just like when he was depressed, once again, he could hardly bear for me to leave his side, and he began to obsess about the future.

One night while talking about his memorial service, he admitted, "I want to go to my own party!" With this discussion, the idea of a "life celebration" was born. We planned the evening, I enlisted help, invitations were sent and Phil chose his favorite charity to benefit from the get together. And, perhaps most importantly, he learned to dance.

We gathered in the living room at night with friends to have lessons. Phil was intent on learning this skill finally, something he had stubbornly refused to do up to this point. He was rather fragile and tired easily, so lessons were limited to fifteen minutes at a time. We spent hours selecting music, then practicing moves while watching YouTube videos, laughing until our sides hurt at how ridiculous we all looked, and laughing even more because we simply no longer cared.

The night of the big event was magical. Friends and family showed up from hundreds of miles away. We saw people from every area of Phil's life—childhood friends, people he graduated from high school with, former teachers, friends from work, and friends we had gone to church with at one time or another. More than a hundred and fifty people packed into a room filled with candles and music and never-ending snapshots from a life well lived. Most of all the room was filled with fun and laughter and memories.

As the song "My Girl" started playing over the speakers, Phil slowly got up and walked over to our daughter, Maria. She looked so pretty in a new yellow dress with her auburn-tinged hair cascading down her back. He held out his hand and asked her, "Will you dance with me?"

Tears gathered in Maria's eyes, and then a luminous smile spread over her face as she said, "Of course."

Phil took her hand and drew her onto the dance floor and held her as they danced. Not the father-daughter dance every little girl dreams of at her wedding, but a dance they were thankful for nonetheless. As the evening progressed, more memories were shared, we all laughed, we all cried, we all thought a little more about what it means to truly live and we all went home that night with hearts more full than when we arrived.

This seemed to be the beginning of the downhill slide for Phil. His health continued to decline. Time and time again we rushed him to the hospital. His pain was out of control as the cancer ate away at his bones, bringing horrible pain. He suffered constantly, and I worried about leaving him alone for any length of time. He moved to using a walker to help get around. He struggled to text or write and began to lose motor and memory skills. He lost weight, developed a stoop, his face took on a grayish cast and in general he began to look like a much older man. He constantly fought fatigue and slept much of the day. His fear increased. The cancer was winning.

It was winning in his mind as well. As the days went by, Phil became increasingly obsessed with making sure I was taken care of when he was gone. He wrote letter after letter making sure his family and our children knew he wanted me to date again. He even hinted—strongly—about who he wanted me to marry after he was gone. He began to cry more often and for longer periods of time. Used tissues littered end tables and nightstands, tumbling onto the floor. Every day felt dark and gray. He was inconsolable.

Each night was the same. I crawled into bed with my husband and tucked him in for the evening. We had a routine. I would get him his medicine and some water for the nightstand and make sure he could reach his glasses and tablet or book. Then I would crawl in beside him and we would talk.

One night we began to talk about heaven. "Do you believe in heaven? Truly?" I asked him. I had wondered if this was what was troubling him—that what he confessed to believe was now being put to the test of reality and he was struggling with the unknown.

He shifted so that he could look at me, and he said, "I truly do believe in heaven, but it's not heaven to me if you are not there. I am going to miss you, and I don't want to go without you."

Tears filled my eyes. I lay my head very gently on his chest and held him. I felt helpless, without any answers to provide comfort. Words seemed more than insufficient, they seemed almost profane. I knew he was terrified, and yet I could do nothing to alleviate his inner suffering.

"I will join you soon," I whispered into the dark. "It will hardly feel like any time at all has passed. I don't know if there is a feeling of time as we know it here once we are in heaven. But one day I will be there with you."

I began to pray. Softly. Haltingly. I wasn't sure what to say, but this was our routine, the one moment of the day I felt held together, the one moment Phil seemed to be at peace. I had no answers, so I did all I knew to do. I held him and I prayed.

And then I sang. Every night for months it was the same, and I did it until the day he died. "I'm kind of homesick...for a country...to which I've never been before...no sad good-byes will there be spoken...and time won't matter anymore." I lifted my voice, and the words rang out, washed over us.

And every night Phil would whisper into my hair, "I'm going to miss hearing you sing."

We celebrated our thirtieth wedding anniversary on June 2, 2014. It is hard to celebrate a special event when you are so vividly aware it's your last one together. "How do I buy a card for this?" was the question I asked myself as I stood at the card rack in Target for almost an hour, wanting this card to be perfect. I wanted Phil to read it and feel loved and cared for. Tears streamed down my face as I searched. Every sentiment seemed wrong, hurtful, painful. We would not have many more years together. We could not look forward to a bright future. We would not grow old as best friends. It hurt to look at them, all a reminder of the things that we would not have, a future we had lost already. I felt robbed and defeated as I left without the perfect card, but later the words came to me and my last anniversary card to my husband was sentiments I scrawled onto a piece of notebook paper.

Phil's gift to me is one I wear every day. On the night of our anniversary he was sick, not feeling well enough to even go out to dinner. We sat on the back porch listening to the song of the crickets as the sun went down and quiet settled over the mountain ridge we live on. The sky faded from that early summer blue to a dusky purple to pink as the sun said good night. We held hands and exchanged cards, neither of which was store-bought, none of our words perfectly expressing the inexpressible of this season of life, but each of us appreciating the effort.

Phil pulled out a small box and handed it to me. I opened it and slowly removed a small velvet pouch. In it I found a simple silver band, hand formed, with a small diamond gracing it. "It's a forever ring," he said. "So you can always wear a ring from me even after you marry again."

Tears stung my eyes, and I felt a burning in my throat. He held my hand and gently slid the ring onto my finger, just as he had thirty years ago on our wedding day. "I don't want you to ever forget me," he said sadly.

"How could I forget you?" I questioned. "I've spent more years with you than without you. I've had three children with you. I've grown up with you. I've always loved you. I always will. I will never forget you." I took his hand and put it over my heart. "You will always live in here. I'll hold you in my heart always."

The rest of June passed as a blur, our days filled with hospital stays. We would come home for a few days; then Phil would plummet again, entering a near comatose state only to pull out of it again and again. He grew weaker each day. We had planned one last trip to the beach with our good friend Matt going along to help us. I feared we would not make it, but Phil begged and the doctor agreed, even allowing him to leave the hospital a little early so we could make our reservations.

We had three beautiful days at the Gulf. We sat on the beach, Phil carefully shaded by double umbrellas. Sipping piña coladas, we dug our toes in the sand, laughed and talked and had moments where life almost felt normal.

One day Phil asked to get into the water. It was a bit rough that day, not like the placid seas we were used to. I agreed if he would allow us to help him and use the floats. And so we traveled to the water's edge, a strange-looking caravan of people and floats, Matt and I tenderly guiding each of his steps through the shifting sands.

Slowly Phil waded in, feeling his way. The small waves knocked him off balance, and it was all we could do to keep him upright. After a struggle we made it past the waves and Phil sighed, lying across the float as he enjoyed the salt water holding his body up, the waves lapping against his skin, the sun shining on his face. He lit up with contentment as he got his wish. "Thank you," he said as he grabbed my hand.

The next morning we went for a walk on the beach. Just the two of us. Matt helped me get him down to the hard-packed sand, to the water's edge where his footing would be more stable. The sand was white underneath our feet, warm and slightly crunchy. Phil leaned against me, bracing himself as he shuffled along. We didn't talk much, but the silence was comfortable. He was wearing my favorite outfit: swim trunks, a bright blue T-shirt we had bought on one of our trips to Hawaii, and a Kauai baseball hat. I looked at him and tried to hold on to this picture of him. I tightened my grip as we walked along, savoring every moment.

That was one of our last good days. Phil began to run a fever that night and became quite delirious and weak, and so we made yet another trip to the hospital, this time in a strange city without our doctors to help guide us. When we finally could make the trip home, he plummeted once again and slipped into a near coma, unable to be roused.

The doctor came in to see him and said, "I don't really understand what is happening. His test results are unchanged. Nothing appears out of the ordinary on the brain scan, yet obviously something has changed." He paused. "Let's watch him for a few days and see how he does. If he doesn't improve, we will talk about what to do—whether to send him home or to some type of facility."

I felt my heart stop at these words. He was talking about moving Phil to our local hospice facility. I wasn't ready for this. If he was sent there, he would never again go home. I swallowed hard, knowing I might have some difficult decisions to make all on my own in the days ahead.

Phil eventually woke up and even improved enough to go home. But this time he chose to do so under hospice care, knowing we had exhausted all treatment options. He had fought. Now it was time to rest, to savor.

The next few weeks were strangely peaceful. He slept a lot, and it seemed as if his battery was simply running down. He lost interest in most things and seemed content just to sit on the back porch, dozing on and off. He moved to a hospital bed, and I slept in a bed next to him, many times falling asleep holding his hand.

One day I took him to sit by the lake. It was a gorgeous, warm day with a soft breeze coming off the water. We were sitting under a big oak tree near the water's edge, and ducks were walking around us. The sky was that pure azure blue that almost hurts your eyes. I glanced over at Phil reclining in his lounge chair and noticed tears running down his face as he gazed out at the lake.

"What's wrong, baby?" I asked, touching his hand. He turned his face slowly to look at me as if waking from a dream.

"I don't see how heaven could be any more beautiful than this." He sighed. "If heaven is like this, I think I am ready to go."

And so he did, passing from this life only two short weeks later, finally at peace in so many ways. He was surrounded by those who loved him most, his children, parents, siblings and close friends. I held one hand and our daughter held the other as he took his last breaths, and I sang in a cracked voice one last time, "I'm kind of homesick…for a country…to which I've never been before…" And then, as he took his last breath, I keened, I wailed, I shook. It was as if something in me was ripped apart when he took his last breath. I will never be the same.

Two years have passed since my husband's death. I've had two years to begin to absorb the reality of being a widow, of doing life alone for the first time in my life. I look back at the woman I was at the beginning of this journey and hardly recognize her. I am so deeply altered. I have glimpsed the eternal while learning to treasure the beauty of the here and now. And through it all, I have grown stronger.

Death is the great awakener. At this point in my life, that is both the good and the bad news. Bad news because I lost some of my innocence and I have had to learn to live with the constant reality of pain and suffering and loss. The good news is that I hopefully have become more compassionate, loving and kind and, in the end, one day, triumphant. The reality is, however, that nothing will ever be the same for me.

And thus, without my permission, a new journey began.

Many have asked why I would choose to write about my journey, to lay my innermost thoughts out there for the world to see—and perhaps judge. Honestly, I have done this in part just for myself. It has been therapeutic to put words to my feelings and struggles, whether those words are profound or not, trained or not, perfect or not. Writing and sharing is a declaration of sorts that my journey has value. I was challenged furthermore by the wisdom of Hemingway when he said, "Write hard and clear about what hurts."[1] And so I began.

The following essays are not instructional in any way. They are not intended to be a source of "self-help" or to be a formal education on the grieving process. They are simply my thoughts, my experiences, and pieces of my journey as a new widow set down in words. They don't form an all-inclusive story; they are more like windows that allow you a glimpse into my journey after loss.

You'll read many of my most intimate fears and questions in the pages ahead. Some essays were written early on, some after months or years had passed, so you will even see how my perspective changed with time and healing. I offer no "right" or "wrong" thoughts, only what was truly happening within me.

I have one goal from this writing, and that is to offer companionship. I hope that as you read, if you too have suffered loss, you might find some company and understand that you are not alone.

Part 2:

The Journey of Widowhood

1
The Fog

It began the morning after Phil died, this dense fogginess I have been living in. It was as if cotton batting separated me from the rest of the world as I was grieving. It also made me feel like I was losing my mind.

I was removed from everyone and everything. Every conversation was hard, each small task terribly difficult. My head seemed to always hurt just a little, and thinking seemed virtually impossible. I found it easier to avoid anything that required mental exertion and just sit. Sometimes I'd find myself curled up on the couch and realize I had been just sitting or sleeping for hours.

Some days the fog isolated me, as I struggled to truly participate in anything around me. Sure, I'd listen to conversations and nod my head, perhaps even answer. But inside I was somewhere far away. Always, always thinking about Phil, about losing him, about the reality that I was a widow, about how I felt, about how he suffered, reliving his final days, and on and on and on. How maudlin. I grew utterly sick of myself, yet I couldn't break out of it; it was always with me.

I would listen to people talk and it was as if my spirit slowly lifted to somewhere far, far away, and eventually I would realize I had no idea what they had been talking about. The rest of the world carried on like normal people while I stayed inside this invisible shell, unable to fully participate in or connect to anything at all. A part of me was always somewhere else, always missing. And from behind this wall, I watched the rest of the world go by.

Sometimes the fog seems like sheer stupidity. I expected a lot of things after Phil's death, but I didn't expect to lose my mental abilities and memory. I struggled to do small things like write a check, remember to pay bills, to grasp concepts and to remember things I had done, papers I had signed. Many things are still a blank to me. I don't remember how I did them, but somehow I did. Everything had to be redone—bank accounts, cable, credit cards, and on and on. The list seemed endless and needlessly cruel.

One day, months later, I found a credit card in my wallet that I had no memory of applying for or receiving. I could not remember anything about it and had to sheepishly call and confess this to figure it out. My body was here on earth but my mind was looking down from a great distance—I was never fully present in anything I did.

Oh, I had moments that weren't bad as others, and over time things have improved. But I am still not myself. I still don't have the energy and drive I once had. Everything takes me much longer to accomplish and wears me out in ways I have never experienced before.

I wonder and worry if I will ever be the same. And I constantly battle the desire just to sit on the couch and be. It is easier and safer there.

2
Longing for a Word

I've heard many people speak of having a loved one appear to them after they passed on. I've even been asked if I have "seen Phil" or heard from him or even received a sign. This is distressing to me because the answer is an almost absolute no.

When he first died, I dreamed about him every night, but they were nightmares. I dreamed over and over again of him lying in that hospital bed, hearing the sound of him breathing heavily and with great rasping sighs over and over and over again, unable to respond or move. It was a scene that repeated itself on an endless loop in my head.

I relived his last moments in my dreams, the screaming and wailing that came from deep within me somewhere, the desperation and sorrow I saw on my children's faces as we were hit with the truth that this was good-bye and death was for real. I don't think this is what people mean when they talk about hearing from a loved one.

For a long time I would talk to Phil before I'd go to sleep. Sometime in that conversation I'd ask him to speak to me in my dreams. I was desperate to connect with him again in any way I could. I don't know if this is really possible, any more than I know if it's possible for him to hear me when I talk or see me from heaven. Honestly, it doesn't seem like it could be very heavenly if we could see the heartache on earth below. But that is not my point.

I don't even know if it is true that people appear and speak to us or send messages from beyond this life, but it shows what grief does to you in that I was perfectly willing to talk out loud to my dead husband in hopes he could hear me and let me know he still loved me. I needed something comforting. Perhaps I was hoping for—and am still hoping for—something sweet and positive after the agony of his death. Night after night I did this, and night after night I heard nothing. Occasionally I still dream of Phil, but it is always a flashback-type dream or he is just somewhere in the dream; never is it meaningful or peaceful. I admit I am jealous of people who feel they hear from loved ones. Whether that is real or not, they are comforted.

All of this does not mean I have not felt Phil's presence since he passed away. In fact, I feel as if he is still very much a part of me, and I think of him constantly, like he is a silent, invisible friend that goes with me wherever I happen to be. But there have been moments where I felt his presence and "smile" in particular ways. Whether that is in my head or is actually true, I don't guess I'll ever know. But it has meant a lot to me.

The first time was the only "spooky" experience I've ever had, if I may call it that. I believe it was within the first week after his death. I was taking a nap in my bedroom. I hadn't slept in there in a few months because I had slept with him in the bedroom where his hospital bed was. So I was back in our bedroom, but alone for the first time.

I woke up suddenly, jerking awake, with the sense that someone was standing over me. I opened my eyes, and just for a moment I saw Phil, like a flash. I was certain it was him. And then he was gone. I do know that there is a psychological term for this, a grief artifact, and it is not uncommon for those that are grieving to "see" their loved one, especially right after a death. But I'll admit that it was a source of comfort, even if it was simply a trick my grief played on me, even though it was just for a flash and he didn't say anything or touch me.

Other times that stand out to me are more gentle and sadly infrequent, although I have prayed and prayed to hear from him more. On our anniversary I sat by the lake and wrote him a letter. I confessed all my failings and regrets as a wife and asked him to forgive me. I told him how much I loved him and how I always would. He was my best friend. I shared what all was going on in my life, with the kids, and things I wish I could discuss with him. I asked his advice. And once again I begged to hear from him, to be assured he still loved me.

I never really had that in any way I envisioned, but I did feel a sense of peace wash over me as I sat on that bench by the lake. I closed my eyes and sat there in the warm sun, feeling the gentle breeze caress my face, and a gentle warmth and stillness descended on me, filling me. I felt him with me.

My first summer without Phil I went to the beach. I couldn't really bear to go to any of our normal vacation spots we had visited in the past. I needed a quiet retreat with no ghosts or memories. So I chose to go to St. George Island, a little barrier island off the northwest coast of Florida in an area referred to as "The Forgotten Coast."

I didn't want to be around crowds, so this was perfect. I arrived in late afternoon to my little house on the beach. As soon as I threw my suitcase inside, I turned and walked right out across that warm sand to the surf, let the waves wash over my feet, drew in a deep breath and an almost alien emotion washed over me.

I realized with surprise that I felt happy. Content. Whole. It wasn't a total healing—I'm not sure that will ever come—but it was the first time I had experienced a truly unencumbered joy in such a long time. I wanted to sing! My soul seemed so light and carefree! I stood there in the surf and soaked it in.

A couple of days later I drove to the end of the island where there is a state park beach. I drove out to the last parking area and then walked east, away from any people, toward the tip of the island. I walked for miles into nothingness but sand and sea, with the sea breeze blowing on my unmade-up face, catching at my hair. The waves lapped at my ankles. I tingled with the awareness that I was alive! It was glorious.

All along the way I found my own little trail of hope. I found sand dollar after sand dollar. Some were floating in the water, some embedded in the sand, others just lying there like an oh so obvious prize. I laughed as I went on my own little treasure hunt, finding drop after drop of hope as I walked along. It was a beautiful day. I ended up with a handful of sand dollars that I clutched carefully in my hands.

A deep peace filled my heart—I knew that Phil would be so happy to see me smile again. In some ways those sand dollars felt like little messages of joy from Phil and God together, saying, "It's going to be all right. There is still great beauty in life." I still have these sand dollars today.

As I approached the one-year anniversary of Phil's heaven-going, I took on a heavier load at school. I knew it was a reality that I needed to finish school and find an actual job—one with benefits and one that paid a living wage. So I signed up for four classes. This was a big deal for me as I still struggled to get things done and to think clearly. I was still in a fog some days, and it was a huge commitment to take on two art classes in a neighboring city, which was over an hour's drive away, and two contract classes I'd do at home. I wondered if I could handle the load.

On my first day of class I was so nervous. I battled my anxiety by dressing in "happy clothes"—a red shirt with bold flowers, one that makes me smile. As I was driving along, I felt Phil's smile. Again, I don't know what is real and what is just our attempt to deal with our grief, but that is how it felt, as if I was warmed by the joy and pride in Phil's smile as he saw me start off for school that first day.

I look for evidence of Phil's presence and love everywhere. I keep my eyes open for it. Sometimes it's a memory that will comfort me, such as the last words he spoke, "I love you." That gives me great peace. I think of him when I see a beautiful sunset or hear the kids say things that remind me of him. Or when I look out into my back garden and see that crazy red elephant he bought me for my last Mother's Day.

Do I wish I could hear more directly from him? Yes I do. Do I think it's possible? I don't really know. I think anything is possible, even things we can't understand. If it happens, I will rejoice. I do know he is with me, carried in my heart, but it is hard to lose those physical touches, the sound of a voice, the grasp of a hand. I'd love to see him one more time and hold his hand and tell him all about my life.

3
Losing My Memories

Grief holds surprises around every bend. I did not expect and could not foresee, all the secondary, somewhat invisible losses that come with losing someone you love, someone that had been such a part of almost every significant—as well as everyday—moment of your life since you were eighteen years old. One in particular has been bothering me lately. Now that Phil is gone, I feel as if I have lost many of my memories.

When I was in my mid-thirties, my grandfather died. I vividly remember seeing my mother and her brothers gather around his casket in that tiny First Baptist Church in Oakman, Alabama, and weep together, holding each other while they cried. After his burial, they told story after story of life with my grandfather, growing up with him as a father, the funny moments and the hard moments.

I remember that afternoon, sitting around in my grandparents' living room with the '70s style gold floral couch and gold carpet, people balancing loaded plates of good, Southern home-cooked food on their knees, conversation flowing all around me. I remember distinctly that I began to feel a new kind of sadness because I realized that as an only child, when my parents die, there will be no one to really remember my childhood with. Those memories will be mine alone, dimmer somehow because they are no longer shared, entrusted only to my memory, which is a bit scary. In that moment I had a foreshadowing of one of the losses I would experience as a widow in just a few years.

No one really talks about this, so it's hard to admit and articulate. It seems a little crazy as I say it out loud. But when I lost Phil, I lost a chunk of my life, not just in his physical absence but in the sense that there were so many memories of my life that I was now the only witness to.

There is now no one to laugh with about our wedding night, no one to remember the excitement of Maria's first steps and how we called everyone we knew and no one was home to tell, no one else to remember the anxious moments in the operating room as each of our three children were born, no one to reminisce and laugh with about funny things the kids used to do and say, no one to remember the amazing adventures we had on our trips to Hawaii, no one to understand certain dynamics in family life and the memories of how they came to be.

Not only is there no one to share happy, precious memories with, but there is no one to share the painful ones with either. No one else who knows how those moments felt, how they hit you in the back of the knees and knocked you down. A huge chunk of my life seemed erased—the only things standing in the way of its extinction are my own fragile memories. It almost seems like events didn't happen or no longer matter in the same way.

Almost all my memories in my adult life were shared with my husband. It is such a lonely feeling to be the sole "rememberer," the sole keeper of the memories, as if I hold them in a box only I know about, only I can unlock. There is no one else to grieve this loss with me either. No one to share with. It's as if a part of my life has been wiped clean, perhaps, or relegated to a corner of my memory that only I can open.

4
I Think I Might Be Crazy...

Of all the ways I expected my husband's death to affect me, feeling more than a little crazy was not one of them. This blindsided me. I had never heard anyone else admit that they felt a bit insane in the wake of losing a loved one, so I worried. A lot.

What in the world is wrong with me? was a question that I asked myself over and over again.

This feeling of craziness is hard to describe. If others do experience it, I'm sure we all feel it in our own unique ways. One thing that made me fear for my sanity were the crying spells that just wouldn't stop. I couldn't get myself together, and this out-of-control feeling scared me and made me wonder if I would ever feel normal again.

One night in particular stands out to me. It was about two months after my husband's death. My youngest son was living with me at the time, and he had gone out of town with his girlfriend. I was home alone for a few days, for the first time really since Phil had passed. On my second night alone, my friend Matt called and asked how I was doing. "Fine, I guess," was my quick reply. What else was there to say? I feel like crap and cry a lot of the time?

But Matt knew me well and invited me over to watch a movie with him and his teenage son. "Maybe it would be good for you to get out of the house," he offered. I accepted, not looking forward to another quiet night by myself. I couldn't really watch television or movies yet, reading left me staring off into space, and everything seemed to be a trigger. But at least I wouldn't be alone.

So I went and sat through the entire movie, staring blankly at the TV but having no idea what was on the screen. When I left, Matt walked me to my car and as I told him good night, I fell apart. I had a total breakdown. I sobbed uncontrollably standing out in the driveway of his house, right on the main street of our little town.

I held on to him and wailed, then bent over and gasped for air. I felt physically ill, as if I were being turned inside out. And I couldn't stop. Without his support I would have dropped to my knees on the concrete.

Matt gently put me in the car and said, "Give me your keys. I'm driving you home." I reached into my purse and managed to locate them and handed them over to him. I cried out loud, great sobbing cries, all the way home. I'm sure I scared him, but he never showed it.

When we got home and into the house, he took my shoulders and turned me to look at him. "Go to the bathroom, get dressed and take something to help you sleep and get into bed. I'll be there in a minute." So I did what he said, robot-like, going through the motions, not daring to look into the mirror for fear of what I might see. I could not bear to face my own ravaged features. I brushed my teeth and took a sleeping pill, then pulled one of Phil's old T-shirts on over my head and fell into bed.

In a few minutes he returned and sat beside me, gently rubbing my back. I still could not stop crying, and as soon as he touched me, the wailing started again, like this sorrow and pain was a wild animal intent on fighting its way out of my body, desperate for escape. I felt like I was possessed by it; I was out of control. I grabbed his hand and gasped, "I think you need to take me to the hospital. I can't get it together." And then he said one of the sweetest things I've ever heard.

"Jan, you are not crazy. You're just grieving.

"Tomorrow will be better," he assured me. He stroked my hair and back for a few minutes, then stood up. "I'm going to sit on the couch until you go to sleep." And he did.

I've thought of this moment many times when I've questioned my sanity as I walked—or more often crawled—through the fog of grief. *"You're not crazy; you're just grieving"* was a reassurance I would offer myself time and time again in the days and months to come.

That "widow's fog" didn't help me have confidence in my mental stability either. I struggled to get things done on time or to concentrate, and sometimes I forgot entire days or events. I could not seem to make decisions. I fretted over every little thing. Should I stain the porches? What color? Should I pay off the house? Should I stay here, or should I move? I felt like a dithering idiot, as if grief had rendered me stupid as well as sad. All decisions seemed hard and emotional and incredibly complicated.

Another thing that really made me question my sanity was the constant feeling that I wanted to run far away. I cannot tell you how many times I thought of just packing a bag and escaping. If our two responses to stress are fight or flight, then mine is most certainly flight. And I wanted to flee with everything in me.

I couldn't tell if it was a good idea or just my response to the pain. I would go back and forth, from *Maybe I need a little time and space?* to *You're just running away from your problems.* It left me so conflicted and unable to trust my gut instincts.

Grief is not something we can truly know until we get there for ourselves. We imagine beforehand that we know what it will be like. We even rationally agree that at some point in our life we will lose someone we love. We expect to feel shock and great sadness. We don't necessarily expect that it will turn our world—and our minds—inside out.

If we really stop to think of it, we might say to ourselves that we don't know what we'll do if a close loved one dies. We could expect that we will be a bit crazy with grief and longing. However, as Joan Didion so eloquently puts it in her own grief memoir, "We do not expect to be literally crazy…" [1]

When I read these words, I laughed out loud because, finally, I had found someone's experience that mirrored my own. I was not alone in my fear that my sanity was a little thinner than I had ever dreamed. Strangely, it made me feel normal.

Grief literally means "to be torn apart." It is no small thing to lose someone we love, to say good-bye, to learn to live without them, to begin again. It incapacitates us for a while, and we must slowly learn to walk again, to live again, to breathe again. Even though we will all lose someone we dearly love in our lifetime, many of us don't have any clear understanding about the very human experience of loss and grief. Like me, so many others think they are "crazy" when, in fact, they are simply human.

We need to realize a great, freeing truth. Grief is natural, an expected response to the passing of a loved one. When we love deeply, we grieve deeply. We cannot manage our grief; we can only learn from it. Even when we feel we are a bit unhinged.

5
You Have To Walk through Grief

This is perhaps the most profound truth about grief that I have learned. You have to walk through it. There are no shortcuts. No expressways that skirt the traffic jams of downtown grief. None. It has been said by more than one wise soul that the only way we can get out of something is to walk through it. We have to march—or crawl—right through the ugly middle of grief in order to ever reach that other side, a place where healing is happening, where our sorrow has gentled into a sweetness that we hold near to our hearts.

I have observed—in my own life, and in others in my work with widow's groups—that while we expect to cry, to be utterly sad and depressed early on, we may begin to wonder as time passes if something is wrong with us. We believe we should be more stoic, that things should not upset us as they do, that we should not cry so much. When we have a bad day, we lament "regressing" or "going backward" in our grief journey.

I will say it again. The hard truth is that the only way out of grief is to experience it. To embrace all the feelings, to face all that unrelenting pain, to explore all my regrets, all my what-ifs, to wonder about all my questions. All of that—while it may not be a journey I want to embark on—is actually good for me. It helps me to face the endless realities of my loss bit by bit. I am coming to grips with a life without someone I dearly loved. How can that not affect me deeply and profoundly?

I remember many times I would text a friend of mine who is a fellow widow. She offered a hand up, a shoulder to cry on, a voice of comfort and experience. I would text her and say, "I think I am having a breakdown."

She would answer, "Just sit and cry it out. It's okay to feel all the feelings."

How I hated this advice. I was sick to death of crying. In between Phil's illness and then his death, I really wondered how I was able to have any tears left at all! I was so tired of myself even, my mopey, "don't care what I look like," "don't want to go anywhere" self. I fervently desired to get on with life, to feel better, to make some forward progress. I wanted to smile again and feel joy. I wanted to wear makeup and not cry it all off. I wanted a normal day with all my heart.

I learned the hard way, as most of us do, that I could not control my grief. No matter how many books I read or how hard I worked, grief has a timetable and work that is all its own. I was not in charge here. I simply had to learn to roll with the waves and come up for air as I could.

While I learned that I cannot wish or work my grief away, I also learned I had something to bring to the table. I had to participate in my own healing. I had to learn not to avoid the pain but to lean into it, to explore it even. I had to want to get better; I had to desire to learn to live again. I had to face my loss squarely and work my way through all the messy emotions that followed. I had to learn healthy coping mechanisms and not cave to the pressure to drown my sorrows in an effort to numb the pain.

In time I gave up trying to fight the tears. I learned to ride in the waves that some days knocked me down, pulling me under, threatening to drown me in their depths. I journaled extensively; I went to see a counselor; I tried new things and went new places; I talked openly about my grief and how it impacted my life. I sought out help from others—Facebook pages, books and support groups. I got outside and walked in nature, focused on strengthening my body. I learned to take "grief breaks" and to take care of my own self.

The journey through grief is anything but linear. I hear people refer to the "stages of grief" all the time. After a lot of research I've come to realize how misunderstood these are. First of all, they were recorded under observations while working with the dying, not the ones who survived a loved one's death.

Secondly, no one who has actually gone through the grief journey would ever agree that there are any nice, orderly steps. How I wish this were so! Wouldn't it be nice to look at your own life and think, *Hmmm, I think I'm halfway through stage two, so I'm almost halfway there! Yay!*

While it would be a great relief to have this set of steps we could walk up in order to reach the light again, instead it has felt more like a tangled ball of yarn, messy and unable to be straightened and smoothed. Most days I feel like I've taken three steps forward, then two steps back. It is a slow journey, one that cannot be rushed, no matter how frustrated we might get. It is a journey of the heart, and it touches on every part of our lives, our souls, our minds. It is all-encompassing.

You can fight it, you can try to avoid it, but it will always catch you. If you stuff it down, it will just come out some other way.

Grief will find you. That's a guarantee.

And I think now that this might be the good news. I realize two years into the grief journey, that grief is not my enemy. It has its purposes. If I had to guess, I'd say that grief will be with me for the rest of my life. Not in the same sharp way as it was at first, but in a gentler way, a constant reminder of the reality of my life that my husband is gone, no longer here on earth with us.

One of the ways I continue to work through my grief is by journaling. About a year after Phil died I took a "Writing Your Grief" course online. One of my entries was to be "Grief Introduces Itself." I was stumped initially, but in the end this is what I wrote.

Hi, my name is grief. I am a sage, sent to escort you from the life you once had into the here and now…and even into the future. I am here to walk with you, speak to you, as you journey through the valleys and vistas of loss.

I know you hate me, that you see me as your enemy, despise me, blame me, detest seeing me coming. I know you wish I would simply go away, but without me there is no way for you to move forward, to adapt and, eventually, even begin to heal.

I know I am ugly and sometimes I come tearing out of the bushes at you when you least expect it, terrorizing you. I see that you have grown weary of that. But I promise I am here to help. What was is no longer, and I am here to help you move to a new way of life. One day you won't need me as much—I'll still be around, but I won't walk so closely to you.

The truth is that there is no way to get from your old life to a new beginning without me. It would help if you could think of me as a friend, someone who has a lot to teach you, show you. I know they are not things you want to know and learn, and some of the places we will walk will not be enjoyable. I know I can be a harsh taskmaster, but in the end it is my goal to help you find peace and acceptance, to squarely face the reality of your loss and still move forward.

I bring you face-to-face with hard things, because if you just walk around *it or try to turn and walk the other way, it takes longer for your heart to heal.*

I will always be with you, but gradually we won't walk so closely together. I will appear less and less, although you may continue to feel my presence. Loss is a reality of life, and where there is loss, I cannot help but follow.

Grief is a march from death to life. And as much as I would like to simply skip it and get on with my life, it's a necessary journey. The only way out is through.

6
I Feel Left Behind

*

Some days it seems as if the world has gone on without me. In the time since we had marital problems and Phil was diagnosed, my life sort of stopped in its tracks. I look around me and realize that everyone else has continued on, the earth kept spinning even while my little world seemed to stand still.

All my closest friends' lives have moved forward, and yet I haven't done much of anything. While my life was being upended and I was busy taking care of my husband and then trying to take care of myself, life moved on, and now I am left behind. It's like a time warp. Everyone else is in 2016, and I am stuck back in 2013.

I had a very vivid dream the other night that perfectly illustrates this point. I was a worship pastor for fifteen years and during this time of my life I made many wonderful friends. I often dream of church, particularly on weekends, but this dream was a bit different. In this dream I was in a large church. The band was setting up for worship. I was friends with many of the band members. There was Bill, who played piano and keys with me, and Dean, who always drummed for me. There was also the other Bill, who played bass behind me for years. And leading it all was my good friend Josh, whom I had worked with for several years. There was even a woman I had a terrible conflict with on a previous team, and she was singing as well. There were many musicians and vocalists onstage that I did not know, but the service was filled with people I used to work with in church.

I sat toward the back of the church and watched anxiously as they played. They had all learned and evolved since we'd been together, showing new talents as they played different instruments and more difficult arrangements. I clapped loudly and tried my best to bring encouragement from my position in the audience. While I was proud of them, I was sad because I was doing nothing, singing nowhere. They had moved on. I was left behind.

As the service ended, I made my way toward the stage, waiting anxiously for them to come down so I could talk to them. I had missed them so much. But one by one they walked right past me. It was as if I were invisible, a ghost of sorts. I called out their names, touched their arms as they passed by. But they could not see me. I did not exist anymore in their world.

And real life mirrors this dream. All my friends have continued on in their course, and I am sitting here wondering what I should do with mine. It's as if time has frozen for me, but in reality the years have passed, children grew up, and people go about their lives.

Yet here I sit alone—seemingly unnoticed most days, sometimes even with my family. People are truly kind, but I have checked out of any normal life activities for so long that I am no longer on their radar. While others have found a new beginning and made new friendships, I have not. I feel left behind. And I don't know what to do with that.

7
Spreading My Wings

About five weeks after my husband passed away, I went on a trip alone. I was so overwhelmed by people talking to me, asking me questions, and having to deal with all the business that pours like an avalanche over you in the wake of the death of a loved one. I desperately wanted to be alone, to not have to talk, listen or figure things out. I needed a break. I was exhausted in every possible way.

I couldn't fathom making any complicated decisions—or any decisions at all—so I took the easy route and called a travel agent and booked a week at an all-inclusive resort in Punta Cana, in the Dominican Republic. She handled everything. I basically just showed up for my flight with a suitcase and my passport and that was about it. It was such a relief.

My family was horrified. They were so worried about me. What did this mean, me "running away" like this? Did it mean I was having a breakdown? My mother was especially concerned and asked many questions, continually offering to come with me. Now, I love my mother, but I didn't want anyone with me. I thought I would unravel if I didn't get the space and quiet that I needed so much.

I boarded the plane in Atlanta that October morning, heading off on my first solo adventure since being widowed. Happy couples filled the plane, laughing as they boarded, the young women sporting "Bride" T-shirts and brand-new, sparkly rings on their left hands. I soon realized that I was on the honeymoon plane! I was the only person on the plane that was not one-half of a couple. Additionally, about 80 percent of the couples were leaving for their honeymoon. This was a painful reminder that I was no longer married, as if I really needed one.

I sat in that crowded plane full of laughing couples and filled out my customs and immigration travel forms. And for the first time in my adult life, I checked the box marked "single." There was no place to clarify, to let the world know I wasn't really single, that in reality I was widowed and still very married in my heart. There was just one truthful option on that form—single. It seemed like a pivotal moment. I felt like I was denying Phil in some way yet acknowledging the truth as well.

It ended up being a beautiful week. The water of the Caribbean was an indescribable color of pale turquoise blue. The palm trees that surrounded the beach swayed in the gentle ocean breezes. My head began to clear, and peace washed over me. I swam, walked on the beach, and spent many hours parked in a lounge chair under an umbrella. Sometimes I slept; other times I was able to read something light. Most of all, I simply rested my entire being—body, soul and mind.

One day as I lay there, I ran across a quote that got my attention. I can't remember where I saw it and, as I've searched for its author and origins, I don't find a clear answer. The words, however, leaped out at me...

"With brave wings she flies..."

I remember writing them down in my ever-present journal that day. In time they would become a sort of mantra I would repeat over and over to myself, in many different ways.

I realized something revolutionary in that moment on the beach. *My life was not over.*

In fact I had a lot of living to do. However, my journey forward was going to require me to be brave. I was going to need much courage to walk into my future, to refuse to live in the past, to climb the stairs into an unknown future, to make decisions on my own, to risk, to enter life again. Life had never been scarier to me than it was after the death of my husband. Vulnerable and afraid, the uncertainty of my future was ever present in my thoughts.

I took this quote and began to surround myself with it. I put it on my refrigerator. I found a leather bracelet with the words stamped on it, and I wore it daily. When I put it on, it's like putting on a piece of armor; I don't feel ready without it. I had an artist draw her interpretation of it, and that picture hangs on the wall at the end of my bed where I can see it as I begin my day.

I took a beginners watercolor class, and one of the assignments was to create a painting from a favorite poem or song lyric. I chose this one and painted a butterfly leaving the dark, transformative time in the cocoon and taking flight, life and love sparkling all around it as it flew.

I got a tattoo on my back of a butterfly lighting on a rose, both symbols of new life for me. I sculpted a bird in clay as I thought on the meaning of these words. I used it to encourage myself to take new steps back into life, no matter how big and scary they may seem. It was my constant reminder to live bravely.

Taking steps forward was terrifying, yet, eventually, they were empowering. Even if it was something as seemingly simple as deciding on a stain color for the porch, once I had overcome my fear and made the decision, it gave me more courage for the next movement forward. I realized I could do the next thing in front of me. I started taking more chances. Eventually I began dreaming again, allowing myself to hope for more than just relief and respite from the grief, but to hope for a new life that was actually good and full of joy.

I learned something else from leaning into this thought: The words we say to ourselves are important. They have power. When I focused on my fears, I became anxious. When I focused on being brave, reminding myself that taking the safe route is not always better and life is full of risks, I felt more able to reach down deep and dig up the courage I needed to follow the trail into my future.

On days when I have been terrified of what is before me; the next decision, of what people in my small town or family are thinking or saying, of taking a chance on a brand-new thing, I remember this. My husband would want me to fly; he would want me to step forward, to be brave enough to build a new life. As I say all the time, choosing to live when I'd rather die is the bravest thing I've ever done.

And one day I'll fly!

8
Who Am I Now?

I now ask myself this question frequently. There is very little about my life that is familiar. I look at it and everything seems barely recognizable. Since there have been so many changes, it is a challenge to define myself at this juncture.

We tend to define ourselves by our roles, by our relationships to other people, perhaps even by our jobs and responsibilities. We define ourselves and describe ourselves by looking in the mirrors that others hold up for us to see our reflections. So who are we when no one is holding up any more mirrors? How do we see ourselves?

I spent all my adult life describing myself as a wife, mother, friend, pastor, vocalist. Before that I was a student and a daughter. Life was pretty neatly formed and defined by these parameters. These were boxes I understood. I knew myself mainly based on how I functioned within these relationships. Other roles were Christian, homemaker (for a while) and, later on, caregiver. One thing these all have in common is that in all these roles, my work was "useful" and fulfilling and each role gave my life direction, meaning and purpose. I was needed for something important in each one of these roles I played.

But now I am no longer a wife, no longer a minister, most of my friends are not near, my children are not around me daily and do not need me in the same ways as before. I am no longer doing the important task of taking care of my sick husband. I am still a Christian but I am struggling hard with my faith, so I don't know how to "own" that role at this time in my life. My faith runs underneath my life like a deep river, ever present beneath my feet, but my legs are shaky, struggling to "get it right" or find comfort in the same ways I used to.

So if I am none of these things anymore—or if I am, but in very different ways—then who am I? I am not sure I have an answer. Since Phil's death I have had several people ask, in a sort of disappointed and incredulous voice, "What do you *do* now?" Although I hate the question, I get it. I barely comprehend my life as it is right now as well. I have moved out into the woods seemingly far from friends, I no longer minister at a church or in other countries, I no longer take care of my husband or my children. What *do* I do now?

Well, I guess, for the first time in my life, I am just Jan. I'm a mom of course, but that looks different these days. I spend time with my parents, who live nearby. I'm working to finish school so I can find a job and support myself. Basically I'm in the midst of figuring what my life can look like, what I want and desire. But still, all these answers are about what I "do."

Why is it that what we do is more important than who we are? I understand. It's so much easier to talk about what we do and who else is in our life than it is talk about who we are. And, while others can help, the only person who can truly hold up that mirror at the end of the day is us.

It takes a bit of self-knowledge and understanding to see ourselves beyond the roles we play, the things we do. We are more than that, thank God. People still can help hold up mirrors, but perhaps they can help us see our innate gifts and the qualities of our hearts, the things that make us shine, instead of only focusing on our activity or what we do to make a paycheck or our relationship to others as our defining qualities.

The changes in my life go far deeper than the change in roles and lifestyle. I once was very innocent, naive even. In many ways I had lived an almost fairy-tale life. I married the love of my life, had three beautiful children, had a job that was my dream come true and I was deeply happy. I was a compassionate person, but I had never been touched by any true trouble in life. Sure, I had faced disappointments. I had been deeply hurt by others at times. But I had never had my world and expectations shattered. My entire reality had never been turned upside down in the way that it has been now.

The person I used to be always believed the best, was deeply sensitive and took herself very seriously. I believed—unconsciously perhaps—that if I did all the right things, then life (or even God) would honor that and life would be good, hopeful and happy.

Some days I really miss that woman. But she is gone now.

I am not pessimistic and bitter now, but I am certainly a more sober person in many ways, vividly aware of the suffering that can strike in an instant, without warning. I am forever changed by that suffering. I hope that these changes shape me into a better person.

There are other changes as well. I feel things even more deeply, as if I have become hypersensitive. I cannot bear conflict or anger; they overload me.

Grief and sorrow have given me the gift of being able to see myself more clearly and realistically, because if there is one thing that grief reveals, it is how fragile you truly are, how weak, how very close to the edge of sanity we can all skate.

At the same time I have come to accept and love myself in a truer way than ever before. I am able to find joy despite my imperfections, or perhaps even because of them. I find joy in the simple things in life now, things I might have overlooked and taken for granted previously. I am less self-conscious and more joyous. I am stronger and more resilient, and yet I am also more fragile and tender. I am a brand-new woman.

So who am I as "just Jan"? I am still figuring that out. I am a woman on a journey from what I was to what I will one day become. I am traveling from "us"—in so many ways as a wife, pastor, mother, even friend—to "me." I am a seeker and I am, at this moment, in a place filled with great questions and unknowingness.

There are few concrete answers for me right now, so I have to be at peace with living with the questions. I will admit it is difficult. How I long for things to be neat and tidy and squared away some days!

I am spending this time learning more about what I love and enjoy in life. I'm learning to lay aside the expectations of others and be true to myself. I'm learning to embrace my unique abilities and qualities and to not be ashamed of my questions or convictions. I'm dabbling in art, chasing sunsets, reading stacks of books, listening to good music, playing with my dog, Ruby, and traveling a little. I'm getting to know myself just as Jan. At fifty years old I'd say it's about time.

I am learning so much in this hard season, always growing it seems. And I am fighting forward—one step, one crawling lunge, one hard-earned inch at a time.

9
What You Don't Know:
A Letter To Those Who Love Me

Dear Loved Ones,

What you don't know and what doesn't always show is how hard everything is for me. Some days I want to stay in bed or sit on the couch and let the world go by. My brain is often foggy, like there is a blanket or thick cloud between me and the world. Even simple tasks seem difficult, as if my mind and thinking are running through thick mud.

I struggle to work at the same pace. Sometimes things as simple as taking the garbage to the end of the road or remembering to look at the bills that are piling up or getting my homework done or caring to buy groceries seem hard, difficult, exhausting.

My brain isn't hitting on all cylinders, as if I am somehow dense, rendered stupid by the dense fog of grief. I hear people talking but often do not comprehend or process well.

I am somewhat apart from the world, as if I'm standing to the side watching myself, but never really engaging as a part of it, my mind endlessly looping on the pain and confusion that is ever present. This makes social events difficult. I want to go. I don't want to be alone all the time, but they exhaust me. I need space to process my loss.

I also lack physical energy. Everything makes me tired. I want to sleep all the time. When I do go shopping or go work out, it takes me forever to recover. My physical capacity is not what it used to be, no matter how much I might wish otherwise. Part of it is that I simply don't care about a lot of things. It's like I cannot muster the energy to get upset or have an opinion. I just want to go to bed and forget.

I wonder if this will ever get better. Sometimes I wonder if I am going crazy or am permanently disabled in some way. Will I always be like this? Will I ever again have the energy I once did? Will I ever again be able to work at full capacity, get things done like I used to? Will I always feel distracted, foggy, in a stupor? Is losing Phil not enough of a blow? Am I forever altered in this way as well?

Another thing that you may not know is that I am having to start all over in almost every way. Not just learning to live alone, but I am also having to somehow rebuild my entire life and this is consuming for me, so confusing and scary. My future seems unknown, the slate totally blank before me. I am paralyzed, unable to make the first mark with the chalk on the blackboard. Each new step forward—a night out with friends, joining a club, meeting someone new, applying for a job, going to a new class seems huge, deeply emotional and incredibly hard.

What you don't know is that it is *harder* to choose to live again than it is to bury myself with my memories. I feel so judged for that—for traveling and dating and trying to make the most of my life. What you don't see and don't know are all the hours I cry, all the days I am utterly hopeless, all the times I have begged God to just let me die. What you don't see and don't know are the wrestlings of my heart that will be there forever, I am sure.

What you don't know is that I am a different person. I can't be the same. I can't go back. This has altered me so deeply that I am not the same person at all. Don't wait for me to get "back to normal," because that is not happening. The old me is gone.

10
Your Faith Must Have Helped You

I've always felt a special closeness to God. I served for many years as a worship pastor, and I taught extensively about what I experienced in my own life—finding communion with our Creator. When I was separated from my husband, I still felt able to pray. Looking back, I'm not sure why, but I still was able to sense God's presence. But after Phil's diagnosis, things were never quite the same. I've stumbled over this reality time and time again.

I know that there were instances during this confusing season of my life that I did not always live according to my own values, my own stated beliefs. I was running from pain, and that was not always pretty. In all this I can freely admit that there were moments that I was not true to my own self, much less to God. It was a dark season—one in which I desperately longed for peace. I don't have all the answers about this. I just know that during our separation I prayed and was able to hear from God and sense his presence.

All of that changed after Phil's terminal diagnosis. Immediately after we were told that there was no cure for his disease and his time was limited, I began to struggle to pray. There seemed to be a brick wall between me and God. If I prayed, I did so haltingly and like a child—praying for protection and healing and blessing but unable to have any meaningful dialogue or feel any true intimacy with the Lord. I cannot tell you how distressing this has been to me, a Christian since the age of nine and a minister for many years.

I would go out on the lake on my paddleboard and sit and cry. Tears would course down my face as my paddle cut through the water, the breeze caressing my skin, oftentimes obscuring my vision so much that I had to stop and sit for a while. I prayed in time with my strokes, each push and pull of my body like a physical plea to heaven. My posture of prayer in those days was either on my face sobbing or paddling on my board. Some days the only prayer I could pray was simply, "God, please don't let go of me." I'd lie out there on the river, facedown on my pink paddleboard, and beg God not to leave me, not to take his hands off me, even when I felt unable to seek him at all.

I have this small wooden cross made from olive wood that fits snugly in the palm of my hand. I would pick it up, feeling the comforting smoothness of it against my skin, and hold it while saying that out loud. "God, please don't let go of me." I'd say it over and over again. It was all I could pray. Holding on to that cross reminded me of the reality that God could hold on to me, no matter how I felt, how turbulent my life was. So I squeezed that little cross tight and prayed.

I have read that it is common in the experience of grief to feel as if our world has tilted on its axis, for what was once familiar and comforting to instead seem foreign and unfamiliar, for old ways to no longer work as they once did, and to have many, many questions. While this may be common, it is still distressing. Where was God when I needed him? Had he abandoned me for good?

In all of this I never really doubted God's goodness. Instead I constantly doubted myself. What had I done wrong? I wondered if I had angered God so much that he had turned his back on me. I harbored a secret fear that he had forgotten me or was angry at me for some reason, that I had ruined my chance of ever having a relationship with God or maybe even going to heaven. I felt unable to talk to God at all about how I felt. To ask for anything unless it was for my children or Phil. And I had no idea how to fix it.

Every once in a while if I knew I was truly alone, I would cry so hard I'd throw up. In the midst of a crying storm, I'd fall to my knees and lie in the floor and weep and wail and scream and beat on the floor in my anger and grief and frustration. I hated my life.

What the hell had happened? Yes. I actually said this to God. Many times, in fact.

I had been serving God, desperately seeking to serve his people, and out of nowhere all this—excuse me—crap hit the fan. Our eldest son attempted suicide and was diagnosed with Bipolar type II and we brought him home to live with us. Phil had a bout of deep depression where he was almost unable to function. I wondered daily if I should drive him to the hospital to be admitted. He was also diagnosed as being Bipolar Type II. We had marriage problems and separated. My mother, who had been diagnosed with Alzheimer's earlier worsened greatly. And then, if that wasn't enough, Phil was dying? How could that be? I was deeply hurt that I had given my best in life and now my entire world was unraveling. Call me childish, but I had no tools in place to handle this—I had no frame of reference. In the depths of my soul I knew that God still loved me in that sort of vague, John 3:16 way that he loves everyone. But inside I felt nothing.

My entire world seemed to disintegrate in front of my eyes. It had been so beautiful, full of dreams come true. Had it been a mirage all that time? No job, no church family, no security in my marriage, no husband, some serious issues with my children and my mother fading away while I watched. Nothing was the same. Nothing was secure. I felt adrift. And very, very alone.

Pain upon pain were stacked high in my life. I couldn't handle it. Looking back, I see it was too much. I understand that psychologically speaking I had complicated grief and what is known as "loss overload", when someone experiences multiple losses close together. While it was kind of comforting to know there was a reason for it, it didn't make the problem go away. Somewhere in the midst of all that I shut down, maybe just to keep functioning.

It seemed that everything I had placed my trust in was gone—even my trust in myself and my own intuitions. Instead of staying firm in my faith during this time, I was like a tumbleweed blown around by winds of change, bad luck, heartache. I rolled around and around and I could not find my bearings to plant my feet on solid ground again. I was hanging on for dear life. I still am some days.

In my naïveté—and because things were so difficult when Phil was sick—I thought some things might get "better" afterward. I thought surely I could not cry much more, my body could not produce any more tears. I was wrong. I still struggle to pray, to believe God longs for me, to feel close to him as I did in the past.

The months following Phil's death—especially after about eight months or so—it often seemed as if I were spiraling downward into a bottomless pit. I still couldn't pray unless I was writing. I continued to panic over going to church. God's presence still seemed out of reach except when I was in nature.

So I did what I could. I chased beauty, sunsets, flowers, anything that spoke to my soul. This brought me some peace. Yet even as I saw this testimony to God's love, I struggled to draw close to him. And it made me feel even more isolated, ashamed and embarrassed—and on occasion, hopeless.

So I pray for myself that God would hold on to me and not let me go. I pray for my children, who live so far away. I pray for my parents and close friends. I pray for direction. But I find it hard to pray for me. In later months I began journaling again, and that has helped. I am able to write prayers when I am unable to speak them.

About fourteen months after Phil's death I went to an appointment, and in talking to someone, I shared that I was a widow and also that prior to my husband's illness, I had been in ministry. She said something that has stuck in my mind and heart ever since. She looked up at me and said, "Well I'm sure your faith has helped you."

I sat there, trying not to cry. The assumption that my faith is strong honestly adds to my shame and sadness because, while I still believe in God and I still have hope for my future, and I am seeking God, at that point I didn't really feel the hand of God or direction or comfort from him.

Grief has been a lonely journey that I have to travel by myself. I know God is with me. I know I am cared for and loved. Yet this is an inward journey of the soul. No one, not even God, can do it for me.

11
Erasing Phil

As time goes by I have a great fear of somehow erasing Phil from my life. Not so much from my memory but from my normal activities. I first encountered this feeling as I tried to go through some of his clothes. I wasn't bothered by giving the kids some of his T-shirts or his dad a few things I thought he might enjoy having. But the thought of giving them *all* away made me uncomfortable. I still can't do it. I sleep in his old T-shirts and unaccountably keep a few of his shirts hanging in the closet even though I don't wear them. I can't bear to totally get rid of his belongings.

I struggled with small items too, such as throwing away his toothbrush or putting away things he used that I never do. Taking his name off accounts and putting them in my name alone seemed like a kind of betrayal, although that seems illogical when I write it down. When I examine my thoughts and heart on this, I think it is because I feel guilty or sad that I am somehow erasing Phil from my life.

I even struggle with how I introduce myself. How soon do I stop saying, "I'm widowed" the first time I meet someone? It seems like such a defining feature of who I am right now. I don't know how to meet someone new and not say it. I wonder that if I don't tell people, I give the impression that I am single or divorced. I hold this somewhat hidden belief that I have to acknowledge Phil still because I don't want anyone else to forget him either.

It's like I carry him around with me all the time, this invisible companion to all that I do. And I am absolutely compelled to talk about it, even though when I meet people for the first time now, they just see me. It's awkward and I really don't know how to handle it.

I vividly remember one day that Phil cried all the way home from the doctor, begging me to keep using the name Owen when he died, even if I remarried. I don't know exactly what he meant, "Jan Owen _____" or simply keeping my current name. When I finally got a bit exasperated and asked him why in the world he'd make such a request and ask such a high-pressure question that I couldn't possibly know my feelings about today, he admitted that he was terribly afraid of being forgotten. Specifically of me forgetting him.

I remember how shocked I was at this. We had been married thirty years and had raised three children together, lived all of life together. How in the world could he believe I would ever forget him? And that is the conversation I come back to in my mind every time I wrestle with what to do with some of his things.

I don't want to forget. I don't want to lose my memories. I want to hang on to them forever. How do I honor the past and still step into my future?

12
The Absolute Unknowing

The uncertainty chokes me. I never saw it coming, this total ambiguity and lack of direction about my future. Some things were clear. I knew I must finish my degree and look for a job, but I had no idea what kind of job to apply for. For the first time in my life I felt no sense of calling or direction about a vocation.

In my twenties I happily stayed at home with my children; in my thirties I joined the ranks of church staff and served as a worship pastor until my midforties. And while there had been crossroads along the path, for the most part I'd always felt a sincere assurance that I was following God's plan for my life. How comforting that was.

Grief wrecks that assurance. It's like taking a walk in the dark. Shapes are dim and the lack of light on the path makes it difficult to know what to do next or to clearly see my surroundings. Enveloped in darkness, I cannot see a path ahead and stumble as I make my way forward. I struggled to make any decision, much less to figure out a new direction for my future. And so here I sit today, forty-nine years old, widowed. No longer in ministry. No longer a wife. My children are adults and no one lives near, so I don't mother a lot like I did before. At a year after losing my husband, I have no clear-cut destination in mind.

People remind me that the possibilities are wide open. I could move anywhere, do almost anything. And I can't tell you how often I have wanted to do that. Move anywhere, away, at least for a time. Sadly, for the first time in my life, I have no clue in terms of direction and calling. I don't know what I should be doing. There are a world of possibilities open before me and yet I am unsure of where to go, what to do, which possibility to choose.

It's like being in a tiny boat in rough seas on a densely foggy night. I'm surrounded by giant waves that threaten to engulf and overturn my boat. I can't see far in any direction and have lost my bearings entirely, so I cannot tell in which direction land lies. And did I mention, I don't even have an oar to paddle and steer with? I squint into the shrouded darkness, but I can see nothing beyond the boundaries of my small boat and the large, crashing waves. No lighthouse, no voice to guide me, nothing. Just waves and fog and darkness. It's terrifying, panicky, frightening.

That sense of calling that had always been so strongly certain in my heart is no longer there—as if it has been muted. It is unsettling. I don't know if it is a call to trust God more, to rest and be still for a season, or if it means I am so far from God that I cannot hear him. I pray that it's not my greatest fear of all, that God is simply done with me. I've let him down, I've fallen short, I've made mistakes and he is all done.

In my head I don't believe this is true. Many people have faced struggles and risen again to serve God with all their lives. I know you don't have to be perfect to serve God or to be used by him. But in my heart I fear that I am somehow different, that there is, in fact, no road ahead of me to follow. That this is it—I will be stuck here forever in this unsettled unknowing.

It is hard to sit in the unknowing.

It is hard to be still in this moment without worrying about or planning for the next one.

It is hard to have no answers for the first time in my life. It is hard to feel rudderless, a tiny ship bobbing about out in the ocean, with no idea where we'll end up and no land in sight. You are at the mercy of the sea and winds for where you may go.

And the tendency, once you are so uncertain, is to just sit down where you are and stay there awhile. You become so afraid of taking the wrong road that you take no roads; in fact, you stop walking altogether. You stop and err on the side of safety and security instead of adventure and exploration. You are afraid to take risks. And that is where I am at. Afraid to take a step because I have no idea what the step should be and I am terrified it will be the wrong one.

Sometimes I have hope. I have to believe that we live into answers sometimes, finding clarity as we experience life and take the next step. Sometimes the answers are not things we can know in the here and now. We must focus on what we can do in the present, what we know currently, and wisdom and insight will come down the road. I know this in my head but often have to remind my heart.

That's where I am today. Trying to take the next known step. Take the next test, write the next paper, finish school, care for myself, do the hard work of mourning. And one day I may live into the answer.

13
How Can I Be Kind to Myself?

I have been seeing a personal counselor ever since Phil's diagnosis of terminal cancer. I say this without shame or embarrassment. I probably owe her my continuing sanity. An aspect of my life that we come back to time and time again is how hard I am on myself. And since grief is difficult enough, she continues to urge me, "Jan, you have got to be easier on yourself."

One day, in utter frustration I am sure, she posed this question to me, "What would it look like if you were to show kindness to yourself?" This question has begun to serve as a guiding light for my grief journey in the days since. I am constantly learning more about what the answers to that question might be. Here are a few things I have learned.

First of all, if I were kind to myself, I would forgive myself.

One of the things I have struggled with the most since my husband's death is letting go of regrets. We had a good marriage for many years but, unfortunately, had a difficult separation that coincided with his cancer diagnosis. I moved home, and we attempted to regain what we once had.

I loved him with all my heart, but some issues that had arisen between us made regaining intimacy a challenge, particularly in the midst of such a stressful time, his continuing struggles with depression and the knowledge that he was going to die. I have had to work hard in order to move on from the feelings of guilt. I have gone to counseling, talked to a pastor, written letters to my husband and talked to God.

I get the same response or seeming answer from them all: "Jan, you are human. We all have regrets. The past is the past; you need to let it go and forgive yourself. Phil knew you loved him, and you took care of him with all your heart." I even felt God say to me from his word, "Forgetting what lies behind and straining forward to what lies ahead..." (English Standard Version, Philippians 3:13).[1]

And yet forgiving myself is a kindness I find hard to show, to accept. I have to do it over and over again. It is the battle of my heart and soul—some days I feel I am overcoming it and other days it hits me full in the heart again and I slide downward into a black hole of the darkest hopelessness and despair.

I would certainly say that forgiving myself is a kindness that would offer healing. Kindness would mean that I stop rehearsing my list of regrets. I would show myself the love, grace and kindness that I so readily offer to others. I would let the past go and walk into the future knowing I am loved.

If I were kind to myself, I would allow myself to feel what I feel without guilt or judgment.

On many occasions I worried about the emotions I was experiencing. Is it wrong to feel anger? Is something wrong with me when I cry day after day? What about the resentment I feel about being the only parent left to help guide our children? What about the days I just have to go back to bed. And stay there? What about when I feel nothing—no hope, no joy, just a gray, flat nothingness?

I suppose some of my worry revolved around the fear that I would never be happy again, or that my level of sadness was abnormal in some way. Grief can be so utterly violent, shaking us body and soul. And yet it can also be likened to this vast empty plain, robbing us of the color of life and leaving the landscape we are living in looking much like a dark winter's day, all black and white and stone-cold.

It would be a kindness to accept my feelings and let them be, knowing that all the emotions of grief are what they are: the response of a heart that has lost someone they loved dearly.

If I were kind to myself, I would understand my limitations and pace myself so that I have time to pay attention to my grief, practice self-care and rest as needed.

Throughout my life I have found it most difficult to show myself grace, often being my own worst critic. It's no surprise that I continue to struggle with managing my own expectations of how I should be doing at this time. I constantly assume I should be doing better—not so much better in my grief, but better in life.

I had no understanding prior to my husband's death of how grief would affect my mental capabilities, my physical health, my ability to concentrate, my energy levels, every aspect of my being. I am critical of my efforts because I am not taking classes, working, and managing the house at full speed. Instead I struggle to get schoolwork done, I am not yet able to handle work and school together, I struggle to exercise steadily, I forget bills, rarely want to be around friends and have dark days where I curl up on the couch and cry and sleep for the entire day. Surely I should be able to get more done by now?

I have wondered at the fine line between this kindness and slower pace and challenging myself to move forward and not drown or bog down in my misery. If I am having a hard day and need to rest, it would be a kindness to give myself what I need. If that is space or some quiet time, then I would do myself a favor and take that.

If I were kind to myself, I would listen to my soul and body and tend to their needs without guilt.

In helping others, I tell them that it's okay at this time to think of yourself, but yet I struggle to practice that. It is a great kindness to pay attention to what my body and mind and heart need—a nap, a walk, a retreat, some fun, etcetera and to actually allow that instead of the constant refrain of "Yes, but you *should* do such and such…"

If I were kind to myself, I would give myself the gift of not constantly worrying about what others think of me and how I am doing.

As a widow I have felt watched, judged even. Am I laughing too loud? Is it wrong to want to go dancing and have a good time? What about if I date? I worry and wonder excessively if others can see how much I love Phil and miss him. I wonder if I am honoring his memory.

If I could be truly kind to myself, I would stop that. I would simply live my life, do what I feel I need to do for my own self, and quit being so concerned and wrapped up in what anyone else thinks.

If I were kind to myself, I would give myself a break and be a good friend to myself.

I would say good-bye to this incessant need to have all the answers about the future today. I would be patient with myself. I would speak gently to myself and remind myself of the truths of the totality of my marriage. I would remember how I cared for my husband, the great heaviness and responsibility I carried in the last few years, and I would call myself good things instead of focusing on my perceived flaws.

I would say encouraging things to myself such as, "Jan, you are courageous and brave. You are strong. You are intelligent. You are caring and loving. You are creative, inventive and compassionate. You were a good wife and mother and love your family very much. You are not beaten down by life. You are an overcomer!" I would cease the constant rehearsal of my faults, my shortcomings and my mistakes and regrets. In short, I would quit beating myself up.

If I were kind to myself, I would take care of my soul.

I would worry less about what I *should* be doing and just do what I *needed* to do.

I would take long walks and naps. I would quit obsessing over all the unknowns, including what my career will be after school. I would give myself the gift of enjoying the "right now" of my life as much as possible. I would be patient with the progress I have made and celebrate my victories, however small they may seem to others.

I would love myself as I am today, not waiting until I have attained some kind of perfection before I can be happy. Even in my grief, I would allow myself to find joy without guilt. I would accept the truth that joy can march alongside sorrow, and I would allow that dichotomy to exist in my heart with acceptance. I would soak in a sunset, linger on the beach, read a good book and savor a glass of wine. I would enjoy today. And I would remember that I was dearly loved, whether I feel I always deserved that love or not.

14
Defending My Grief

Something has been nagging at me all day. A dart has lodged in my heart and has formed an ache that won't go away. I can't seem to shake it. I couldn't figure out what it was—why I was carrying around this feeling of melancholy, why I stayed on the edge of sadness and tears.

I finally traced it back to a conversation I had with an acquaintance. It wasn't a bad conversation, but I realized in looking back that it left me feeling misunderstood. It made me a bit defensive as if I needed to stand up for my grief and the multitudes of losses being a widow had brought, so many of which are invisible to others. While they might not be losses others are aware of, they have impacted me so deeply that moving forward at times has seemed impossible, and my only goal has been to hang on in the midst of the storm, hoping not to be swept away in the grief and chaos.

I remember reading a book by a widower where he described the impact of losing his wife. He said at first he thought it was like having your home totally remodeled, stripped down to the studs. In time, however, he realized that metaphor would not work. Instead he likened it to the house being burned to the ground and wondering if he had the energy to build another.[1] That is exactly how widowhood has been for me.

In this conversation I was lamenting how very few ministries I see for widows, how invisible it seemed us widows are. He kept pointing out the food pantries, people who mow lawns, counseling, etcetera, and I kept trying to explain that those were admirable and nice but not targeted enough—that women and men who lose a spouse need more than someone to be help around the house, although that is appreciated. What they need is support and encouragement to learn to live again.

He said, "Well, maybe someone whose husband has been deployed would understand." I was shocked and answered more vehemently than I should have that while that has to be really hard, having your husband gone, even for months on end, is not the same as having your husband die and leave you forever. I'm sure my tone of voice startled him.

I became frustrated, and in looking back, I realized I had to defend my grief and losses. That happens frequently when I try to share the invisible losses—I just want people to try to see and attempt to understand. Not because I want attention. I do, however, want my pain to be acknowledged and not skipped over and certainly not dismissed.

I want to be seen in the reality of where I am. To gain a bit of validation that, yes, it's been hellishly hard. Instead of someone arguing and debating with me about what pain in this world is worse, or why things might be worse or how it can't be that bad, I want someone to say, simply, "I'm sorry."

I'm sorry that no one came around to help in the yard after Phil died.

I'm sorry that hardly anyone showed up with food.

I'm sorry that most of the multitudes of people that surrounded Phil, including his family, disappeared the moment he took his last breath or after the memorial.

I'm sorry that you felt alone.

I'm sorry that church has offered virtually no attention to the plight of widows and no church reached out to you.

I'm sorry that you had to deal with so many things and carry so many huge weights all by yourself.

I'm sorry your future seems so uncertain. I know all of that must have been and continues to be difficult. I am so sorry.

Don't try to debate. Don't say, "Well, at least you know he's not in pain." Or worse yet, "At least you have life insurance." Don't try to put my pain in a pretty white box with a pink bow and make it more palatable. It's ugly and harsh. Don't try to diminish the reality of my pain or compare it to someone else's. Just believe me when I say it has been hard, the most incredibly difficult and life-altering thing I've ever walked through, and have compassion for that. Care. Hear me and don't look away from the pain in my eyes. Put your arm around me and give me the gift of touch and see me where I am. And say, *I'm so sorry, Jan. You are loved.*

This is what any of us who have been devastated by loss want—to have our story heard, our pain seen and acknowledged, and to feel compassion and a loving hand on our shoulder. We want to know that someone out there cares that we hurt.

15
It Takes Courage To Keep Living

One Thursday evening I was upstairs in my "junk room" trying to put up boxes of odds and ends that have sat there in this space that was intended to be my office ever since we moved into this house in November of 2011. Almost four years. Many of the items are sentimental in nature, such as letters and photos, memorabilia, things I cannot bear to part with but have no idea where they now belong.

While I was up there, surrounded by my late husband's books, awards he has won, memories of thirty-one years together, items from my children's growing-up years, I ran across one of the few scrapbooks I have ever completed—one that captured our twentieth anniversary trip to Maui. It was our first time to visit Hawaii, and as I slowly looked through it, reading the notes I'd written, reliving the moments contained in those pictures, I cried.

Now, this is nothing new. I cry often these days. But this was different. There was some sadness, of course, but it was a comforting kind of crying. There in that room, surrounded by memories, I felt secure. This was known. Familiar.

My new world feels foreign to me, strange, with nothing familiar to hang on to. Here, in the midst of these memories, I felt close to Phil, I felt connected to a life that was at one time as comfortable to me as my current life is alien. I wanted to camp out up in that little dormer room and stay there forever, cuddled up with my security blanket of memories. I even had the thought that I'd be happy living out my days here on earth like this, surrounded by the memories of better days with those I loved. Memories of a time I can never again have or recreate.

In that moment there was a strong temptation to turn my life and home into a memorial and shrine to what was. To stay safely within the walls of this comforting and comfortable place. Don't date, don't worry about calling or vocation, focus on making ends meet. Stay focused on remembering all the beautiful memories of what was once my reality, since I obviously cannot have what I expected and dreamed of for my future.

As I sat there thinking on this, I had a vivid memory of a passage from Charles Dickens' book *Great Expectations* in which Miss Havisham keeps everything in her home as it was on her should-have-been wedding day.[1] She continues to wear her wedding dress, the dining room table is still set with a wedding feast, cake molding, cobwebs adorning everything. She even has all her clocks stopped at twenty minutes till nine, the exact moment she was jilted by her fiancé. Her life and home became a monument to a past she could not let go of—the expectations and dreams that were never realized.

In a less dramatic sense, I could relate. Sometimes that is what it seems even society expects of me as a widow—this building a monument to my husband who is no longer alive and camping out at the foot of it. In this way I show that I truly grieve and love my husband. It proves me to be a "good widow."

In the year since I lost Phil, I have faced this expectation and temptation time and time again. And to be honest, I have come to believe that living in the past is the easy way out. At least for me.

It requires much more courage to keep living, to embrace even small moments of life again in the midst of feeling all this grief. To start over. To press onward. To fight forward. In fact I'd go ahead and call it a true act of bravery—this choosing to live again when I'd rather not.

The reality is that my life has been turned inside out and upside down to the point I don't even recognize it—I no longer serve in ministry, so I am not a minister anymore. I am no longer a wife, and my children live hours away, so I am not a mom in the same way I used to be. My grief is for much more than losing my husband. I am starting over in every way imaginable except where I live—and who knows, that may change one day as well.

Starting over is hard. Forging a new path is risky. It is terrifying to have no answers and to have everything on the horizon be unfamiliar and strange. Honestly it's easier to sit at home on the couch, ensconced in what I once knew. It is easier to live in the midst of my memories instead of having the guts to make some new ones. To sleep in a shrine to grief and loss instead of waking to the beauty of life.

As I sat in the floor of my extra room upstairs, surrounded by memories of what was and dreams of what might have been, I became convinced Phil would be heartbroken that I would choose that path. He would want me to enjoy life to its fullest instead of taking the path of least resistance.

But I was aware that it was hard. Hard to face the disapproving opinions of others when you don't meet their expectations of what a grieving widow looks like, even when they themselves have never been widowed. It's hard to leap out into the unknown when you are struggling each day to get up out of bed and even care. And it's hard to make special new memories without the person you loved. That has stopped me more times than I'd like to admit, this idea that I cannot enjoy something new and beautiful because my husband is no longer alive to enjoy it either.

So, courage. What does that mean? The dictionary defines it as the quality of mind or spirit that enables a person to face difficulty, danger, pain, etcetera, without fear; bravery. Braveness, audacity, heroism, daring, determination, grit, spunk, spirit, tenacity, fortitude, valor, dauntlessness. This is what it takes to fight forward. It's not for the faint of heart. It's easier to stay where it's safe. But who ever said the best path back into life was the easy route?

The bravest thing I've ever done is choosing to live when I'd rather not.

16
One Year In

On the one-year anniversary of Phil's passing, I wrote the following essay and posted it online to share with his friends.

* * *

I've been trying to think of what I might say to mark this day—the anniversary of the day that literally took my breath away, the day I held Phil's hand for the last time, kissed him one last time, watched the incredible heartache of my children as he took his last breath, had to say good-bye. Watching someone you love pass from this life to the next is one of the most heart-wrenching, steal-your-breath things I've ever experienced, and as this day comes, it is hard not to be overwhelmed by flashbacks and images of the end.

These images flash through my mind unbidden, without permission, when I most want to be at peace, knocking the breath out of me again and again. I don't know what to do with those memories, with that pain of losing Phil that is a constant companion—sometimes worse, sometimes better, always there as a low, throbbing bass note underneath the activity of everyday life. I don't want to forget what it felt like to lose Phil, however. It seems that might be yet another loss.

I do know this. I am ready to learn from the pain of it all, everything we went through. Pain is a great teacher—it can make us wiser, more compassionate, more self-aware. It can change our perspective on life.

May my suffering not be in vain...

Even with that being said, I know without a doubt that Phil would not want any of us who loved him to cling to that pain, to wallow in it, thinking this will honor his memory in some way. Yes, it is there. No, we sometimes cannot shake it and probably will carry it with us all of our days—it will continue to shape us and inform our lives. How could it not?

A great loss does that to you. It changes you. It stays with you. But Phil would want us all, in answer to his death, more than anything, to live our lives as fully as possible. He would want us to have new adventures, hug our loved ones, laugh out loud, be happy, dance, literally take time to smell the roses. He would not want us to focus on his death but on life instead. To appreciate the gift of life. To remember, in fact, that we are loved.

I read a beautiful Jewish prayer that goes like this: "God, let me not die while I am still alive."[1] This prayer, this plea resonates in my heart. I've thought of getting it tattooed on my arm where I'd see it every day.

It has been the greatest challenge to me in the past year simply to choose to live. I would say that choosing life has taken the most courage of anything I've ever done—the grit-your-teeth-and-force-yourself-forward kind of courage. I have wanted to sit on the couch or lie in the bed and let life pass me by. To quit. And many days I have done just that.

In time I realized that it was not respectful of my own life or Phil's to waste my days, to be ungrateful for the time I have here on this earth. It honors no one for me to "die while still alive." And so I fight forward—I try new things, I go on trips, I laugh, I force myself to go to the gym, I face my fears, I study for classes, I go on a date, I dream of a happy future, I live with hope—an imperfect hope, but hope nonetheless. Every one of these things is a step forward of courage and a step toward life.

Life. May I never take it for granted again.

So tonight remember with me a man who was intelligent and funny in his very dry kind of way, a man who became a husband at nineteen and a father at twenty and never batted an eye, a man who always was intent on serving others, a man that fought his own struggles but kept going, a man that loved a little adventure down an unknown road, a man who loved his children, who loved me—even when we didn't deserve it. Remember a man that loved his coffee, pizza, college football, the LSU Tigers and the Alabama Crimson Tide, Disney World, and all things geeky. Remember that precious man and don't focus on his pain but on his life. Honor him by choosing to live.

I leave you with a toast. I hope you will take a moment tonight to join me. Just mute the TV or pause before bed and raise your glass with me. I am not Jewish but felt this traditional toast expressed my heart at this time. I envision Phil raising his glass—be it filled with sweet tea, coffee or champagne—with all of us and saying loudly, "L'chaim!"

To life. To life, my friends. Live it boldly and fully.

17
Fighting Forward vs. Hanging On

At the one-year mark now I seem to be in the midst of a struggle—the struggle between moving forward and hanging on. It is not that I am over my grief in any way. I still do a fair share of crying, I still have days where I feel good and angry and want to curse at the world, "Why me?" There are plenty of days I go to sleep and feel hopeless, thinking to myself that I'd be okay with going on home if God would assure me he'd take care of my children.

But ever increasingly there is a desire to live again, to fight for what is next, what is to come, although I still don't know what that is completely. There is a desire to not feel the sadness all the time, like an undercurrent of my life that never leaves me.

I long to feel some freedom—freedom to laugh and sing and be in love and dance and run barefoot down the beach, freedom from worrying about what the world thinks of me as a widow, freedom even from worrying constantly about how my moving forward will upset my own children. I long to feel the freedom to just be me and to live again.

And yet…on the other hand I am afraid to move forward. I am afraid to let go. I struggle with guilt. I don't know how to really be "just Jan."

I don't totally understand it, but there is always a tinge of guilt as I take steps back into life, even though I desperately desire to make some progress. I don't want to I forget Phil, and as some of the sharp edges of my grief fade, I suppose there is a deep-seated fear that it means I am forgetting him as well. If I am not angry and crying all the time, does this mean I don't love him as much as I used to? If I make room in my life for another man, does this mean I am abandoning Phil, even though he is already physically gone? It's crazy-making, I tell you. Crazy-making.

I went to the counselor one time and was deeply upset. When she asked me why I was crying, I shared that I had been sleeping great and was doing pretty good and I didn't know what was wrong with me. She laughed quietly and said something truly profound though oh so simple. She said, "Jan, just be grateful. Don't feel guilty. Be grateful."

Why are we hounded by feelings of guilt as things getting easier, as we begin to enjoy life again? I think at times we see a correlation between the depth of our grief and how much we loved the person we lost, so when we are feeling some happiness and joy, we panic. We not only worry that for ourselves—that our grief connection and hence our love is fading—but we also fear that is what others will think as well. "Oh, she's already dating again. I can't believe she forgot her husband that fast!" Or when we laugh with a group of friends or choose to go out and have fun, we worry that people are thinking, "How can she laugh? Doesn't she have any respect for her husband?"

Now, the truth is that I don't know if people are really thinking these things or not. But either we have heard it said about others in the past—or perhaps even thought it ourselves about people before we personally went through the heartbreaking experience of being widowed—or we've had hints of it directed at us and so we begin to be self-conscious about it. At least this has been true for me. I finally had to realize that when I change my life in order for it to make "others" happy, the only person it truly impacts is me. And this is my one and only life to live.

But there is still an internal struggle, a fear that if I start truly enjoying life again, I am committing a crime of the heart against my late husband. There is also a fear deep down, although it sounds absurd when vocalized, that somehow I will forget him or erase him. That my bond with him will loosen. That the grief makes him feel closer somehow. And truthfully, I am not ready to have the events of now begin to replace the memories of him. I'm not ready.

So I walk a tenuous line—trying to keep my eyes on the horizon with great hope, and yet always holding the memories of my first true love deep in my heart, close to me always, every moment of every day, perhaps even cherishing that pain.

18
How Would You Love Me in This?

How would you love me in this?

I have asked myself this a thousand times, a million times even. What would Phil say to me about this? How would he respond to me in my grief? How would he love and comfort me?

Phil, before you died you urged me to live again, to go ahead and date again as soon as I wanted, to marry again, to not wait to jump back into life. But it has been so incredibly debilitating, this losing you.

I could not jump; some days I could not even crawl or stumble or move at all. I've been exhausted and beaten, yet filled with a longing to move forward and live again. I've stayed so caught up in remorse, regret at times that I was tempted to wish for death as well, yet I also longed to forget what is behind me and move on to a hopeful future.

I know what you'd say about that. You'd tell me to let it go, to not waste my life staring backward. *Learn from it and move on, Jan.* You'd tell me that you understand that it was hard, that I had a difficult path with many obstacles and responsibilities to deal with— mostly all on my own.

You'd urge me to be kind to myself—to think of myself—for once in my life.

You'd remind me of how precious life is, and you'd encourage me to enjoy it, to laugh in wonder, to be amazed, to not be ashamed to feel joy—or love—again. I think you would be my biggest cheerleader as I travel on this unwanted journey.

You would be proud of me—of my going back to school, of how I have tried to care for others out of a new compassion borne from my own loss and determination to not give up.

It would disappoint you mightily if I had done what I wanted to in those early days, which was to lie down and go to sleep and not wake up. Your life was cut short and this saddened you; how sad if I gave up on the opportunity and life I have been given.

On hard days you would draw me a hot bath and add some bubbles and bring me a glass of wine and encourage me to take a break. To just be still. Then you'd rub my back and tell me to rest.

I know you'd encourage me to do what I need to do. Of this I am certain.

You always admired my independent spirit and never stood in my way when I dreamed a dream or wanted to try something new. In fact you usually encouraged each step I took in life and cheered me on along the way. How I wish I had appreciated this more when you were alive! I took that for granted!

Our home meant so much to you, but if I wanted to move to get a fresh start, to go exploring around the world, or to move to the beach, you'd be okay with that! You'd help me pack! (Well, maybe a little. You actually sucked at packing to move!) You would urge me to follow my dreams, to love again, to write that book, finish my degree, take that trip, make that change, learn that something new.

Perhaps the way you'd love me most of all would be to encourage me to step forward into life without fear. Every time I have a new experience, I carry you with me. I now live for both of us.

19
I Became My Own Hero

It takes a certain toughness to move forward while grieving. I have often referred to my grief journey as a fight for my life. In any given moment there are so many images in my head, so many negative thoughts, so many remembrances of failure and mistakes and pain and hurt, that it is easy to get bogged down, to long to lie down and go to sleep and never wake up. I felt unworthy to be the one who lived. I couldn't figure out how to fight with the negative thoughts, to turn them off or, at the very least, to turn them down so that I could function.

In time I realized that if I was going to survive, I had to develop some mental toughness, something I have always struggled with because I am such a super-sensitive soul, and because I feel things so deeply.

I realized, maybe for the first time in my life, an important lesson—that I didn't have to accept the damaging words and images that entered my head and heart; I could actually fight back. When I heard hurtful words people had said about me echoing in my head, I could decide not to accept it, not to receive it, and not to internalize it. It was like being offered food and realizing I had the choice to say, *No, thank you, I don't want to eat that.*

Toughness is required because it requires toughness and courage to speak up, to act, to lean into the truth and the good memories, to decide what my own mind would dwell on and what it would not. It takes toughness to get up each day and move forward, to not cave in, to not go back to bed, but to choose to live.

Choosing to live when I'd rather die has been the bravest thing I have ever done.

As my college graduation began to loom closer and closer, I became more and more anxious because I wasn't sure what career to pursue. I was terrified I could not support myself.

I kept waiting on a door to magically open, for a ministry position to become available, perhaps, or a friend to offer me a job. This time? Silence. Crickets. Nothing. Nada. Was God finished with me? I felt abandoned.

One day I woke up and realized that no one was going to save me. Now that probably sounds ridiculous. Yet I had never in my adult life applied for or interviewed for a job. I had always been offered positions. Doors had simply opened, even when I was not knocking. The way had always felt pretty clear, as if the path was magically laid out before me, but now it was so foggy. Everything felt dim and confusing.

I realized that I was going to have to pursue what I wanted one step at a time. I firmly believe that action brings clarity. As much as I wish we could map out our entire journey while sitting cuddled up on the couch underneath a warm, fuzzy, comforting blanket while sipping a cup of hot tea, I believe we have to choose to move, to follow the terrain of the land, so to speak. In other words, we have to take a step forward to find light for the next step, and the next and the next.

In time I decided to apply for graduate school, to pursue a goal of becoming a counselor. I was terrified to even begin the process. When I learned about all the testing, the clinical work for licensure, how few people are actually accepted into the program, I thought long about it and almost said, *Forget it. That sounds too hard.*

I was afraid I couldn't do it, that I would fail. I was afraid to do something so far out of my comfort zone. I was afraid of making a mistake. It's taken some firm talking to myself to put the positive thoughts in my head that need to be there. I realized I was going to have to be tougher to move forward into scary and uncharted territory.

It takes toughness because the grief journey is like a hard, muddy march through enemy territory.

You're carrying so much weight, the terrain is unfamiliar, you feel you are likely to be ambushed at any moment, and you have no idea what to expect and you'd really just like to give up and die, or at least fall asleep on the side of the trail and stay there. This was not the hike—the journey of a lifetime—you signed up for.

To keep putting one muddy boot in front of the other moment by moment has required the most courage of anything else in my life.

To not give up, to decide not to just to sit down and set up camp in the nearest seemingly safe place, not to go hide behind a rock somewhere for the rest of my life, not to turn around and run for my life in the opposite direction, but instead to march—or crawl—determinedly onward into what feels like the vast unknown has taken a great deal of grit and bravery. I don't mind saying that. I've surprised myself, if I'm honest. I had no idea I was this strong, this determined.

This is no luxury cruise, folks. This is a down-and-dirty march out of death and into life.

I recently read Cheryl Strayed's book *Wild*, in which she chronicles her experience with losing her mother, then kind of losing herself in her grief and finally finding herself again as she solo hiked 1000 miles on the Pacific Crest Trail through California and Oregon. I felt like her hiking journey was a good pictorial analogy of the journey of widow's grief.

She starts out as a total novice hiker, not even sure what to take along or how to do it. She makes mistakes, is scared, thinks she's losing her mind, loses her toenails, yet valiantly (or stupidly in some people's eyes), she marches on, even after losing her boots, making do with her current reality (flip flops and duct tape) instead of quitting. I could relate.

In the grind of walking forward, step by painstaking step, she found herself again. In time she threw out things she didn't need, she altered her expectations and said good-bye to the expectations and opinions of others as well. In the end it was just her and the trail.

And she survived, walking through the grief as she climbed hills, marched through deserts, plowed through snow and fought the biggest demon of them all—her own self. And she often wanted to quit—multiple times every day.[1]

So it is with widowhood. It takes a lot of spunk and grit and—on some days—steely determination—to march on.

To fight for your life.

To forge ahead when you are terrified of the future. To choose to trust and love again. To allow grief to shape us into our best—

instead of our worst—selves. To allow our pain to catapult us to a better place in life.

To learn to live again.

20
Scattering Ashes

Today I took a journey. Last fall I read a book in which the author shared the details of spreading her late husband's ashes, and it struck me right in the heart. I realized I had to move forward in this regard. I finished the book, snapped it shut and immediately booked a flight to Guatemala. It was clear what I had to do. I must take some of Phil's ashes to El Yalu, the Mayan village in the hills of Guatemala near Sumpango where Phil requested some of his ashes be scattered.

For some time we had made an annual trip to work in Guatemala. We helped local missionaries, worked in schools, served in feeding centers, repaired primitive homes, installed latrines and built stoves for families. Most of the work we did centered around the small Mayan village called El Yalu. Phil was so happy there. He even spoke of retiring and moving there to work. I saw him smile in Guatemala more than anywhere else.

And so I proceeded. I started making necessary arrangements. I e-mailed a Guatemalan friend to help me when I arrived. I then booked a flight and hotel. I contacted the funeral home for help in dividing up his cremated remains so I could take them with me. A sense of relief was immediate—as if a weight had lifted from my shoulders. I had a plan. I hadn't realized how heavily this had weighed on my heart and mind, to not have this done, one of Phil's last requests.

Sunday I arrived in Guatemala, having safely gotten Phil's ashes through a lengthy security search on the US side. I was staying in Antigua very near the Central Park. Within an hour or so I was once again practicing my stilted Spanish, assuring everyone who asked that, "Mi espanol is muy puquena. Lo siento" or "My Spanish is very small. I'm sorry." But still, like every other visit, I managed to make do. Between their limited English and my limited Spanish and the sign language we sometimes threw in, I managed.

I wandered the streets of Antigua, so familiar yet, in some ways, seeming like a memory from another long-ago lifetime. Memories of our last trip here washed over me as I walked the same streets, seeing scenes in my mind from our time together in this place.

I will admit that the first afternoon was challenging. I didn't want to curl up in a ball and weep, but I felt undoubtedly sad. I felt like my heart was bombarded with memories, mostly good. I had one vivid memory that left me feeling ashamed and deeply saddened, as if I were a no-good, low-down human being and not much of a wife.

I remembered on one of our trips Phil and I got into an argument. I was upset about something that he thought was no big deal. It hurt my feelings that he didn't take me seriously. I had to teach that night at a local church while Phil and the rest of our group all went out to eat. I was frustrated as we parted ways. When I returned to the hotel, a beautiful jade necklace was waiting for me, along with a sweet love note. He had bought it from a nice jewelry shop, so it probably cost quite a bit.

As I relived that night, I thought of all the ways I had failed him and I felt so small. I wished for the millionth time for a do over, another chance to be a better wife to him, to appreciate him more, to not be stupid in some ways.

I remembered shopping in the markets, wandering through the rabbit's warren of booths brimming with colorful goods, "You buy, pretty lady?" echoing from the vendors. We had our own little ritual. It was always me buying and Phil paying—and carrying.

We also always, always stopped at the bodega to find something fun to take home. I really did not enjoy the grocery store experience in Antigua, but Phil loved it. He had so much fun roaming the aisles, seeing what was available. I remembered many rambling walks in the dark along the cobblestone streets at the end of a long day's work, and how much Phil loved it here.

The next morning I rose early and my friends Oscar and Karla picked me up and drove me to the small mountain village of El Yalu. This is the village we worked in for many years, and it sits in the hills that surround the city of Sumpango. As we rode up the mountain, I held tightly to the jar that contained Phil's ashes, my body swaying back and forth as we drove around winding curves and bounced along unpaved roads.

As I gazed out the car window at the familiar yet slightly different landscape we passed through, so many memories rushed back. We passed old men leading bony brown cows and boys with loads of firewood on their backs. Women and young girls in traditional dress passed by, wearing the *huipiles* (traditional blouses) of their villages, the long skirts, dark heads adorned with loads of laundry, cornmeal, or water and their backs weighted down by babies tied tightly to their bodies, little round faces peeking out at the world. And the dogs. There were dogs everywhere. They faithfully followed their masters, trotting unceasingly to the fields to work and back again. It was a never ending parade in and among the never-ending, beautiful green hills of Guatemala.

When we finally arrived, Oscar asked me where I wanted to scatter Phil's ashes. There was no obvious place, no beautiful overlook with some good, clean area to do this. I had thought about the question before coming, so I told him I wanted to hike up the path behind the houses and do it there, in a spot Phil and I had taken a picture years before. I remembered this path as a trail, easy enough to navigate. But when we arrived, it was like a gully that had been washed out—there was no walking; it was a climb. At the same time it seemed like a small highway with people coming and going constantly. When we'd been there before, we had never seen another soul!

We began to climb, me holding the container carefully, afraid I'd drop it and it would shatter right here in the path amid the cow dung, where everyone would trample on it. It had been one of my biggest fears, that they'd take his ashes away at customs or not let me bring them or something, and now I was afraid I'd drop them. I couldn't bear that thought, so I climbed with one hand and held the jar firmly to my chest with the other.

Finally, breathless from the climb, we reached the place we had taken the photo years before. It looked different now. It was grown up more, the view was not as good, plants were thick along the trail. I felt a bit awkward as people traveled up and down passing us, but I pressed on, pushing down my anxiety. This was what Phil wanted.

I had brought along my small Bible and I read from it the same scripture read at his memorial service:

And I heard a loud voice from the throne, saying, "Behold the dwelling place of God is with man. He will dwell with them and they will be his people, and God himself will be with them as their God. He will wipe away every tear from their eyes, and death shall be no more, neither shall there be mourning, nor crying, nor pain anymore, for the former things are passed away." And he who was seated on the throne said, "Behold I make all things new…" (Rev. 21:3-5)[1] **

I sobbed as I read the words, my voice shaking, my eyes blurring, making it difficult to see. I thought of a day with no sorrow, no tears, no pain, and I thought that this was where Phil now is—he will never again experience pain or sadness; he is completely whole. The words "Behold, I make all things new" really struck me as prophetic—a word for new beginnings, both for Phil and for me.

Karla moved closer to me and put her arm around me, holding on to me as my body shook. I wanted to sob loudly, to break down and give in to the tears, but I was out in public, on the side of a mountain in a village in Guatemala, with people walking past with their cows. It was surreal.

I held my sobs in the best I could. I took the jar of Phil's ashes, and I gently poured them out into the brush there by the trail. The wind blew the ash back onto my hands, and I felt him touching me once again. Every few seconds I'd have to move for a few cows to go by—up this gully that seemed to go to nowhere but obviously was as heavily trafficked as a major highway. Guatemalans are unfailingly polite, so every time someone would pass, they would greet us with *Buenas dias* and nod and smile. I am sure they were puzzled at what we were doing just standing there in the trail on the side of a steep hill.

After we had to move out of the way five times I found myself holding back laughter. It suddenly seemed kind of humorous. My emotions vacillated from sobbing loudly to wanting to bend over and laugh hysterically. As I had envisioned this moment, I never imagined all the cows and people traipsing through our little ceremony. I giggled to myself as I considered how amusing Phil would find this and could imagine his face, creased with laughter. I could see him in my mind's eye, dressed in his work pants and old T-shirts, as happy as I've ever seen him there in the streets of El Yalu.

Finally I finished and asked Oscar to pray. We held hands and said a prayer of thanksgiving for Phil's life, his work, his love. We prayed for our children, for me, for that village that Phil loved so much, a place where a part of him will remain forever, deep in the soil of El Yalu. I suppose we call many places in our lifetimes "home." I know that for Phil, El Yalu was one of those places.

I felt peace. I had done what he asked. I may have failed in many ways, but I had done my best for him in this case, I had honored his request for some of him to remain always in Guatemala. I felt sad, empty, missing him terribly and yet lighter and at peace.

Rest in peace, Phil. Can you see me here, in this place we loved, you loved? Are you smiling?

* * *

After my visit to El Yalu, I came back to Antigua. I dropped off my belongings at my hotel and went out to enjoy the beautifully sunny day. I had not eaten breakfast and was thinking I'd just wander around and find somewhere to grab something light.

I had noticed a nice jewelry store across the street from my hotel several times, and I often thought about going in to look around. I hesitantly entered, and a nice woman named Patricia helped me. I explained I was looking for a piece of jade jewelry to commemorate my visit here, to remember when I came and left my husband's ashes in one of his favorite places.

She spoke to me about the meaning of the different colors of jade. I spent quite some time trying different ones on and thinking about what I might want. I was finally drawn to a ring of dark green jade, representing the earth and new life. I put it on my finger and wore it proudly, knowing I would forevermore be reminded of Phil and our times in Guatemala when I wore it.

After lunch I went searching for the entrance to the ruins of St. Joseph's Cathedral. I had passed it many times and was curious to see what was inside. I wandered in, paid my 8Qs, and roamed around a bit taking photos.

While in the main section of the cathedral ruins, I noticed an almost pure white dove up on one of the cornices. It had one small black spot on its body. I took a photo of it, and then it swooped down, walking around just a couple of feet in front of me. I froze for a few seconds, watching it carefully. I slowly raised my phone to snap a few more shots. As I was taking the last one, it flew up in the air, and I captured that moment.

I don't know why, but this moment was deeply significant to me. I can't define what it meant, just that it seemed I had experienced a visitation of some sort. I am not sure I can assign a particular message to it.

I only know I felt visited. And at peace. Phil was home.

21
Angel on an Airplane

Sometimes God sends an angel. Maybe not a literal angel, but an emissary of sorts, someone to speak hope into your life when you are least expecting it.

On the plane ride home yesterday to Huntsville, I sat next to a woman who was obviously of Latino origins. We were laughing together about how the plane was so cold. I shared that I was returning from Guatemala and it had been beautifully warm and sunny there and I was not enjoying the cold of being back home. She got really excited and said, "I am from Guatemala! That is my country!" She told me she had lived in the US for thirty-five years but that she still misses her homeland.

We talked the entire flight. She was curious about my trip and asked me why I had visited Guatemala and what I had done while I was there. I explained that my late husband and I had made the trip many times and worked in a tiny village up in the hills, El Yalu. She asked a lot of questions, so I explained to her how Phil seemed happier there, more at ease and relaxed, with nothing more stressful to do but build things with his hands to help others, how emotional it was to go back to visit without him by my side, how the village had changed over the years, how I had missed working there.

She asked, "Well, where did you scatter his ashes?" I kind of laughed and told her that it had been a bit difficult to find what seemed an appropriate place, but that I had finally settled on this path that overlooked the village, somewhere we had a photo of the two of us there that is one of my favorites.

I shared about the never-ending procession of people, cows and dogs that wandered by as we tried to have a little quiet moment, and how, in the end, it made me laugh. I shared my belief that Phil would have found it quite amusing! I got my phone out and showed her the photos I had taken from that morning, and she exclaimed over each one.

She asked about the work I had done, and I was able to share how much I enjoyed my time as a worship pastor, then as a missionary, but explained that now I was just a student trying to finish college and figure out God's plan for my life once again. She gently led me to share what I loved about it, and I told her that I felt at home helping people; it gave me pleasure and a deep purpose. Even though I felt a bit conscious saying it, I shared that it was what I felt called by God to do.

We talked about different ideas, about how hard it was being widowed, about dating even. She had so much wisdom to share. As I sat there talking to her, I wished she would adopt me so we could have a continuing relationship. She was warm and comfortable, encouraging and positive. My time with her was a gift.

At one point near the end of the flight she took my hands in hers and looked me in the eyes. I felt she was looking into my soul as she said, "I'm so proud of you. You are continuing to live! You have such life and light about you. God has put a special fire in you!"

I just sat there, stunned. Tears gathered in my eyes and I wondered, *Could it be true? Could God have new things for me, more ministry? Could he still use me?* In all my life, one of the most certain things I have known is that I was called by God. Right up until my life blew apart. Since then I have not felt this certainty, because I know I did not always respond to the challenges as I should have. I quit seeing myself as "called," and this upended my life almost as much as being widowed. It was a loss at the deepest part of my being, at the core of my identity.

Even with all my doubts and fears, I have recently caught glimmers of that calling again. I wish I had a clear word, a peaceful clarity. I just know that unworthy as I am, God is somehow, in his great grace, not finished with me yet.

This woman seemed like an ancient prophetess to me, speaking life into my soul, over me as we sat on that tiny airplane zooming through the sky that day. I did not know her, yet I believe God used her to speak truth to me. She was able to see in me something I had lost sight of myself. I would go so far as to say she—a woman who did not know me—was somehow able to see straight to my heart, her gaze uncluttered by pain and heartache.

I truly believe we are more than our past, our mistakes, our questions and lowest moments. Good people can make mistakes, have dubious judgment, be overwhelmed by their circumstances and run from difficulties. History—and the Bible—certainly show us this. What I have struggled with is not defining myself by my mistakes, not feeling that I am totally unworthy now to ever be used by God again. And, if I am honest, if I am not called to minister, then I honestly do not know who I am anymore.

But this Guatemalan woman with warm eyes and a gentle, encouraging presence saw more than my mistakes, my self-doubt, my pain, my grief. I'd like to think she saw my heart and my desire as she took my hands in hers there on that plane, right out in public, and spoke, "You are a strong woman. God has made you strong to deal with all these problems. He has put a fire in your heart that cannot be put out, and he has big things for you to do, people for you to help. You have a light to shine."

Then she leaned down and kissed my hand gently and whispered, with tears in her eyes, "Thank you for loving the people of my country. There is so much poverty and sadness. Thank you."

Tears ran down my face.

I felt as if I had been visited by an angel.

22
What I've Loved I Cannot Hold

I have learned, to my sorrow, that the life I have loved is not one I can hold on to. It is gone like a vapor, and it almost seems like a long-ago dream at times. In the midst of many losses, losing Phil was the event that—finally—totally wrecked me. I have had to learn that so many things I built my life on, that I counted on, that I defined myself by, are not things that can be held forever. They are temporary at best, a moment in time to be savored perhaps, but here on earth they do not last.

We think they do. We assume that when "we" build a good life, a beautiful family, have a job we love, share a happy life with those that love us, that it will be forever. But it's not. It can't be, can it? Isn't change in all its forms inevitable? Loss is a part of life, however much we'd like to deny this. And therefore, so are both pain and change. It is unavoidable. We cannot hang on to all that we love.

As I write this, I think it sounds so defeatist. So negative. But I don't write it with that attitude. I write it from acceptance, a sense of reality I did not have before my husband's illness and passing.

Sometimes life pries our fingers open from people and things we love. Life is just hard, things happen, people make choices, life marches forward, changes occur and, yes, our fingers are metaphorically pried open.

We have to learn to let go of so many things! Of regrets, mistakes, past unhealthy relationships and so on. But also— sometimes—we must learn to let go of things we love and expectations that we have held dear our entire lives.

As parents we have to open our hands and let go of our children as they grow into adults. As children, eventually we will have to let go of our parents as they age and leave us. All of us will probably lose friends we love or even jobs we were deeply attached to. This is life. Yet when we are in the midst of great happiness, we cannot see it. We believe our sweet world will stay the same and last forever. Oh, that this were so!

In the last few years I have had to let go of many things I loved. Leaving my job as a worship pastor was truly difficult. Talk about prying your fingers open? Well, mine were clenched very tightly around my career and this place I called home. It wasn't just my job or calling; it was my personal church as well. And so the change ripped me apart.

In addition to just a paycheck or a church, I lost a set of friends. They still love me, but we are not together much now so it's still a very real—and deep—loss. I also lost how I saw myself, how I identified myself. I was a pastor, a worship pastor. I sang for my supper in many ways. I loved it. I loved my team. I had wanted to be a minister my entire life. And now I was not. So what was I?

About the same time my youngest child left for college. I experienced empty nest. My children are good people, but they make decisions I don't always agree with—and I am learning that those decisions are not mine to make. They are adults now, and I cannot make sure that they are okay at every moment, I can't make them take care of themselves or determine how their life will turn out. They're responsible for their choices now, and I must let go of my need for control. I must trust them with their own futures.

My son and husband both experienced severe issues with mental health disorders. My husband and I separated, which was one of the lowest points of my life. I lost feelings of security in my family and marriage. I feared for the lives and sanity of my husband and son, and on some days I feared for my own sanity as well.

This is not at all something I expected or was prepared for. This was not how I wanted or envisioned my family to be. Yet it was my reality, and I couldn't keep fighting against it. At some point I had to reach a place of acceptance in order to deal with the reality of it.

When I felt like I couldn't handle one more thing, my husband was diagnosed with terminal cancer. We reunited, but things were different. There were so many pressures and emotions. And then, quickly, he was gone. My security as a happy, whole family—my image of who we were together and even who I was as a person— had to be relinquished.

I had to learn to accept what *was* instead of yearning for *what was not*, what once was true but could never be again. I had to learn that I could not remake what I once had, nor could I rebuild what my life once looked like. It is futile to keep trying to recreate what is gone, what is now our past. I had to look forward to prepare for and find a new and different future. One that did not look like what I had planned at all.

One big thing I had to learn to let go of were my expectations of what I thought my life would look like, how I had envisioned it would be. I thought, like so many others, that Phil and I would grow old together; our children would live nearby, marrying and having grandchildren.

The death of that dream, that expectation, was deeply painful for me. I had to let go of others' expectations for me, to begin to live my own life. I learned to honor my one life, because it is the only one I have. I cannot live it according to others' expectations, and I cannot live it in the past. I have to let those things go, loosen my hands, quiet the angry struggling of my heart, release what I thought would be. This, I've come to see, is the pathway to peace. Learning to let go, say good-bye and start anew.

My former life was beautiful, but it is no longer current reality. I had to accept that in order to find some sort of peace. And I didn't reach that place overnight. I still kick and scream in anger and protest some days, yelling, "I want my old life back!"

It is hard to let go of all we hold dear, isn't it? To say good-bye without feeling guilty. Letting go has seemed to me to be even slightly disloyal, as if I am saying my years with Phil did not matter, or I don't care about them. Nothing could be farther from the truth.

I am coming to see, however, that in order to survive, in order to have a healthy mind, even, I am going to have to let go, to say good-bye, to the way things once were.

I hate this.

More than anything I long to turn back time, to be given a second chance, to be right back smack in the middle of my sweet, safe little family in a church that I loved, with a good marriage that felt endless and totally safe, feeling certain of who I was and what I believed. I don't have any of that anymore. It's all gone.

But also, as I look back, I realize that who I am today doesn't fit into that particular picture anymore. My old beliefs and the "givens"

I took for granted in life no longer serve me well, they don't fit, like a coat that I've outgrown and now feels too tight across the chest and in the shoulders. I don't really even know how to communicate it, I just know that I am utterly altered and there is no going back.

And so I must learn to let go. To say good-bye, to open my hands, to release what I cannot control and what I obviously cannot keep. It is no longer mine, and I cannot have it back.

This may be the ultimate pain, to realize that the loss goes so much wider and deeper than even one single person. And there is not a thing you can do about it—no amount of fighting, anger, tears, yelling, lying on the floor and kicking my heels, begging or demanding will help, although God knows I have done all of that. In the end there is only one option: open my fingers and let go. I truly see this as the path of peace, although it is not something I'm particularly happy about.

Along the way I realized that different could also be happy. I had to realize that my life could be beautiful again. I had to lay down the expectations or even the desire that it would be like it used to be or how I had always expected it to be. I could not embrace the now or move forward into the future without doing this, without learning to let go. Which I hate. Which hurts. Which is hard.

We cannot hang on to the things we love because the truth is, there is so much in life and, of course, in others that we simply cannot—and should not—control.

Yet somehow, along the way, we might discover a new normal, a new beginning, a new way of being, that is beautiful and delightful as well. And, in doing so, reach a place of peace.

23
Happy Anniversary, Baby:
Thoughts on Our Thirty-second Anniversary

I woke up this morning, the morning of what would have been our thirty-second anniversary, with words on my lips, memories in my heart. I have often wondered since Phil died if he can hear me talk to him. I tell him things all the time. I don't know if he can hear me, but I'm not ruling it out. I still talk to him.

Today I woke up and thought "Happy anniversary, sweetheart. I miss you and I love you. I'd love to hear an 'I love you' from you today please." Then I waited. Silence. I guess since Phil was a man of few words when he was alive, it shouldn't surprise me if he's quiet now, too. Yet I felt him with me, words or not.

What a strange day—how do I celebrate this occasion? I can't let the day go by without acknowledging it, yet I'm not sure how to celebrate it either. Is celebrate the right word? I don't know. Just like so many other things about grief, there's no good rational and easy and clear-cut answer. I don't feel capable of a normal, go-about-your-business day, but the truth is that until you arrive on these days, you don't know what you feel like doing anyway. So I try to prepare but keep it flexible. And I've learned to lay all expectations aside.

One thing I never expected or understood about grief is how, as time goes on, as life begins to invade again, as we allow it to seep back into our lives and it runs, at first like little rivulets, over the parched, brown grass of our hearts and then expands into bigger and bigger streams watering our souls, oftentimes joy and sorrow will march hand in hand. Both will be true for us. We will carry them both inside. And that's okay. It's okay—and good—to be happy. And it's perfectly and beautifully human to be sad. Both are our truth. Both are our reality.

I miss Phil every day. For a long time my most vivid memories were of his last year or so, the harshness of his last days, the pain he was in, the constant tears he cried, the terrible heavy anxiety that I carried everywhere. But lately I've remembered more of the things that were happy and good—hearing him laugh loudly as he watched some stupidly juvenile show like *Malcolm in the Middle* or *My Name Is Earl*, watching him do his rare "touchdown dance" when Alabama or LSU made a particularly spectacular touchdown (he saved this for extremely special occasions!), seeing his excitement over making a pizza in his pizza oven or roasting his own coffee beans or seeing him interact with the kids.

This morning I thought about our wedding day. Two extremely young kids getting married without a clue. I didn't think of sentimental things, however. I thought of the funny things. I thought about our honeymoon night in that crummy old hotel room at Mount Cheaha State Park and how Phil said it was the "longest drive of his life" to get there.

I remembered how he would often joke in later years, "You wanna revisit the scene of the crime?" (I always laughingly declined!) I remembered how we got up the next morning and decided we'd go back to our apartment, although we didn't have a bed yet, just a mattress on the floor. And I remembered how nice it was to be naive and clueless—we were so innocent.

Phil and I had a lot of good years and a few painful and difficult ones. Perhaps that is just the truth of love—it's not always grand. Sometimes it's gritty and full of humanity. We fail in our love in so many ways.

I never know how to approach this day. So as I lay in bed this morning, I asked Phil a question. "What do you think I should do today?" And this time I feel I heard an answer. I heard him say very clearly, "Live."

24
The Rebirth of Me

When our spouse or someone we deeply love dies, we try so hard to regather the tatters of our former life around us and hope it will be enough, hope we can remake what we once had, somehow stitching around the hole left by loss. I see this in my life; I see it in others.

We fight for this. We desperately want things to be like they once were. I've also heard it said repeatedly that this is impossible to do. When our futile attempts to stitch it all back together in the old way fail, we become angry and frustrated. Eventually we are forced to face head-on the reality that all our anger and pretending and living in the past will not resurrect the beauty of what we once had.

One of the works of grief is to bring us from the place we were to the place we are, to transition us, no matter how ugly and painful that transition may seem, to a new beginning, a new version of ourselves, a new life, a new normal.

But how do we do this? Is it something we can create, or is it a metamorphosis that slowly happens to us as we walk the path of grief? Is it a change that happens as time passes and we naturally must begin to live into all those new beginnings? As we once again begin to embrace life, inch by inch?

Perhaps it is a bit of both. It is a natural occurrence but also one that requires our participation. And by taking those little, seemingly insignificant baby steps, we can partner with the passage of time to enter into a fresh and hopeful beginning.

But there's such a quandary to this, isn't there? In widowhood we are given a new beginning we did not want or ask for. We just want our old life back, but sadly, it's gone. We must take those building blocks and build something entirely new. We resist. We fling our blocks away in disgust. We shout and demand what was once ours to return

Honestly I sometimes feel that society puts the pressure on us widows to stay in our former life out of "respect" for our late spouses, keeping our life just as it was as a way of honoring them. We may feel judged by some when we take steps forward, as if we didn't love our spouses enough and are now just leaving them behind. The truth is, we can't keep the life we shared with our spouse. No matter how hard we fight it, what is before us is a blank slate, a new building lot, and it is totally empty. The old reality is crushed, broken. It no longer exists.

So we are handed this new life we didn't want. And we are constantly given the chance to write a next chapter of our story, to build a new home for ourselves. Life keeps intruding and giving us chances and opportunities to step forward. Unexpected friends, new hobbies, even putting things in our name that used to be in our husband's, traveling to previously unfamiliar places, having to handle responsibilities, learning needed skills for the first time. All are invitations that knock on our door again and again. Invitations to life, a fresh way of being, a brand-new us. Invitations to say "yes" to life as it just keeps coming.

That is one thing about life. It continually moves along. And we will eventually step back fully into the flow or be left on the riverbank. I have to admit this truth. The riverbank feels much more comfortable and predictable and safe than the actual river itself. Stepping out into the flow of the river is frightening and scary, and we aren't sure where we'll end up. It's so tempting to just sit on the mossy bank and watch life pass us by.

At some point we have to get to know ourselves again, to begin to dream our own dreams, something that seems flatly impossible early in our grief journey. I realized in the desperation of my own grief that I would have to learn to take care of myself—and that no one but me could do it. Yes, there are a million other things to deal with and there is always another person that will need us. I came to know in the agony of grief that if I didn't use this opportunity to be kind to myself, to grow as an individual, as just Jan, I would never be able to handle the road ahead.

I would not be able to help my adult children. I would not be able to help care for my mother as her Alzheimer's progressed. I would not be able to finish school and prepare for a new career. I would not be able to find a job and support myself. If I didn't take care of myself now, I would not be able to live life fully later.

I often tell new widows that it is okay to be "selfish" at this time. Most women I know live for their families. They may work, but they are caregivers. They put their families above all else—themselves included. Oftentimes they are responsible for others in their lives as well. In the wake of such a loss, we can still feel pulled in a million different directions, listening to all the different voices, hearing needs—and opinions and expectations—come at us from all directions. As we hear these voices, as we have advice shouted at us from the right and the left, we may feel guilty when we ignore them, often doing what others want at the expense of honoring our own lives.

Only we can save ourselves. And in truth, it is the only life we can actually save. That may be one of the biggest lessons I have learned through this grief journey—it is my responsibility and privilege to live my one holy life. It is my life to live. Yes, others will have opinions. They may even have expectations. But in the end I must be true to myself and listen to my inner voice, my own heart speaking to me in the midst of chaos.

This has been painfully difficult for me. I am a people pleaser and certainly do not like to be judged and talked about. I really hurt when I know that I have disappointed someone. In the midst of trying to please the world, I woke up one day and realized I wasn't pleasing myself. I had to look deep within my heart and ask myself a big question: "What do you want to do, Jan?"

As I began to step back into the river of life, I made a list of things I wanted to do. Ideas I wanted to explore. Experiences I wanted to taste.

I tried some art classes. Photography, watercolor, ceramics, writing. All these things have opened up new places in my heart, offered the opportunity for new friendships and relationships I might never have encountered before. They also opened up never-before-experienced challenges and ways to express my life and heart and even my grief.

These are mostly unfamiliar and heretofore untried things for me—or I am pursuing them in new ways, with a new focus. They are opening doors to unexplored places within me places previously untapped.

I won't lie to you. It has been a bit frightening as well. I suppose all new things are in some way. I would stare at that blank piece of paper and I would feel anxiety gather in my stomach as I looked at the paints, thinking, *What in the world am I doing here?*

I felt like a kindergartener making a gift out of clay for my mother in ceramics class. Yet in the end it was its own form of therapy. A chance to play in a new way. And it was empowering.

No, I did not become an artist through these classes and endeavors. But I did learn new things about myself, and I had a chance to express my grief and longings in newfound ways. I promise you that if you try new things, life will offer you chances to learn and grow.

I also wrote and I wrote and I wrote. I have filled probably a thousand pages or more with my thoughts and feelings on this grief journey. I have explored my questions, written angrily of what I hated about my new life, begged and pleaded with both God and even, at times, with Phil—and yes, even began to explore new dreams of my own. Writing is something that healed my soul as I participated in my own therapy, the path forward. It is now a priority of my day, a practice I have committed myself to, for my own sanity.

I have traveled to new places, challenging myself to do things I have never done on my own before. I have gone to concerts, finding music that speaks to me in this time. I have focused on strengthening my body and spending time outdoors. I am finishing school and dreaming of what might be next. I have gone to counseling, read dozens of books and focused on the healing of my own heart.

How have I been reborn at the core of who I am? I am more courageous than before. Life is uncertain in brand-new ways at this point. At first I was terrified to take chances or even to make simple decisions. I have learned to live in the moment more, to take one step at a time, and to consider options for my life I had never dreamed of previously.

I am not as concerned about the voices of others now. Don't misunderstand me. This is still a struggle. I don't like to disappoint those around me, and I love to know people like me. As grief has stripped me, knocked me to the ground, I have found I simply do not have the energy for anything else but survival and figuring out my own life. I cannot care as much as I once did. I can no longer participate in drama.

I am more of a realist now. I don't trust as easily in the aftermath of sickness and death. That's the negative side, I suppose. I have lost so much of my naïveté. Somewhere along the line, my rose-colored glasses got knocked off and smashed into a million pieces.

I spend more time alone. I need more time to myself to work through what is happening in my heart, to adjust to all the loss and changes and to sit in silence and just be. Noise confounds me, upsets me. I can only handle so much.

I see myself more clearly now. I am deeply humbled by my experiences. I have learned from my many mistakes, I've—sadly— had to confront my own selfishness. I have been stripped bare and left lying facedown on the floor of life by a multitude of losses. I am able to admit to myself—and slowly, to others—my own imperfections, bad choices and weaknesses.

On the other hand I also see and accept my strengths and beauty more willingly. Without apology. I see more clearly what I am good at, what gifts I may have to offer the world around me. I know the value of my own life and have fallen in love with the beauty of my own soul, something I have wrestled with for many decades. I am who I am. Not perfect by a long shot, but a woman getting stronger, more honest, less controlled by fears, becoming more true to myself every day.

I still have questions about what it looks like for me to be reborn and yet still honor Phil and our past together. How do I remember the past without living in it any longer? How do I honor my past life with my husband while setting an entirely new course? I am still looking for some answers.

Maybe I haven't been reborn quite yet; perhaps I am still in the midst of a beautiful "becoming."

25
Choosing To Live

I've often struggled to explain how totally encompassing and life altering the loss of my husband has been. Not to whine, but my life has been filled with loss in the last few years.

Nothing is the same anymore.

Not where I live, work, go to church, my family dynamics, my roles in life, my marital status, ministry or my family support system. Additionally now I must prepare for and begin an entirely new career to support myself.

All of this to say that I have a simple choice: I can crawl determinedly into a new life and future, or I can sit down and die and remain in a past that I cannot regain. As my son so wisely pointed out to me one day, "Refusing to live won't bring Dad back."

Since I have only one life and it is mine to live, I will choose to live it fully and with purpose. In fact—I will say it again—choosing to live when I would rather die is the most courageous thing I have ever done, the hardest battle I have ever fought.

It has been the fight of my life, for my life.

Sadly there has been some judgment about these "steps forward." Whatever that might be—traveling, a new purchase, the possible move for graduate school, and, most particularly, dating.

Most people have been kind and encouraging. I appreciate my cheerleaders so much. But some have said things that were hurtful and I feel most of those people made assumptions about me and my intentions that showed they had no understanding of my life or my heart. I admit with sadness that I myself have made assumptions about others' actions in their grief in the past, and I have had to apologize for that.

I hope my words bring enlightenment. My steps forward in no way show any disrespect to the life I shared with Phil, my life as it once was. If one day I move out of this house, it will be so that I can be where I need to be for that time in my life. If I go to a party and have a good time or travel to someplace I've always wanted to see, then good for me; I have chosen to engage in life again and make the most of mine. If I go to graduate school, it will be so that I can proudly provide for myself in a vocation I feel ministers to and helps others.

And when I began to date, be assured it was not a step I took lightly. Most of all, be assured that dating in no way indicates I have "gotten over" losing Phil or that I no longer think of him or love him. Nothing could be farther from the truth.

I think of Phil multiple times a day. He is always with me. I carry him in my heart. I often laugh at things he would find funny, and I still cry because I miss him so much. I will love him forever.

In all honesty, my feelings for Matt, the man I am now dating, have nothing to do with my feelings for Phil. I didn't understand how this could be until I experienced it for myself, but it has been like my heart has enlarged so that I am able to love and remember and honor Phil, while also loving again here on earth. What a gift I consider this to be.

It was important to Phil that I continue to live—to make a difference in this world, to experience the joys life can hold and to find love again if possible. He was particularly emphatic about that last point. I remember a late-night conversation after we learned his condition was terminal.

We were lying in bed and he said, "Jan, I want you to marry again if you want to. But I just want you to promise me three things."

I cuddled up close to him and listened expectantly, nodding my head.

He went on, "Number one. Don't marry someone so much better than me that they make me look bad. Number two. Don't marry someone who just wants your money or the house. And number three. Don't marry one of those musicians you love to hang out with."

I laughingly reminded him all my musician friends were engineers and computer geeks like him! He had a great sense of humor about it, but it was clear he worried about my future. He was much more concerned about me being alone than I was.

Phil would be the first one to tell you that he would never see my dating to be disrespectful to him or a sign that I did not love him enough. He would never see my steps forward as an indication that I am "over" losing him, something I am not even sure is possible.

I will always be Phil's widow no matter what happens in my future. And I think I knew Phil better than anyone else in the world—I know for a fact he'd be proud of me for choosing to step back into life in every single way.

I prayed that prayer that I mentioned before that was shared by a Jewish rabbi. I prayed it for months and months. It is still something I go back to often.

"*God, let me not die while I'm still alive.*"[2]

While I have the gift of life, may I not waste my days, may I recognize it as a gift, may I open my heart and eyes to the beauty and love in the world and may I be willing to feel the pain and walk with others in their darkness as well.

May I not give up, may I build a new life brick by brick and may I continue to fight forward inch by hard-won inch each and every day.

Let me not die while I'm still alive.

26
A Different Kind of Faith

"Once upon a time you had it all beautifully sorted out. Then you didn't."[1]

This quote from Sarah Bessey sums up my faith journey as it has intertwined with my grief. I wrote earlier about how I struggled to pray and feel God's presence in the wake of my husband's illness and death. I can't emphasize enough how distressing this has been to me, and how—with all my "knowledge" as a teacher and minister—I had no idea how to fix it. I was simply too weary and discouraged to figure it out. It felt too hard.

Everything I was experiencing were things I simply had no precedent for, no experience to pull from. Yet I continued to pray in my stumbling, halting, desperate way, often through my writing, and almost always through a waterfall of tears.

I didn't want to end this book without touching on the topic of faith once again, because to me it has been a deeply important place of wrestling. Whether you hold any religious beliefs or not, grief can impact the lens we are accustomed to viewing our world and life through, as well as our faith. I wanted to share where I am today, two years post loss. If pressed for a concrete answer, the best I'm afraid I could give you is to say that I'm still on that journey. I'm still living with my questions.

Aren't we always? We oftentimes—in those good, sweet times—don't realize the truth that we never fully arrive. Everything feels clear and firm when things are going well. Answers seem obvious, the path simple. We are certain we know how we would respond in each and every situation.

I still have so many questions and so few answers. I have learned to be at peace with that. Perhaps—and this is radical—God is not only okay with us having questions, but maybe he actually appreciates them.

We emphasize blind obedience as faith, but I think if we are truthful, we all wrestle from time to time with what we believe and how it squares up with our day-to-day reality, particularly as we encounter great grief and pain. Faith seems better described to me as believing in God while holding out your questions and fears anyway, trusting that he will meet you there in the midst of the unknowing. Faith is not certainty; it is believing even in the uncertainty.

We see throughout scripture people who brought their questions openly and honestly to God—David and Job are two examples, as is Jesus. Christ himself exclaimed in a moment of great pain and agony, "My God, my God, why have you forsaken me?"[2]

I have come to a place of peace with my questions—and even with the lack of hard and rigid answers that I used to think I had all figured out. I am now willing and able to reexamine my own conclusions from the first half of my life. That thought would have frightened me at one time. Now the idea doesn't feel threatening; it's simply what I must do.

In the most painful moments of my life I have come to know God even more as a God of compassion and empathy. He does not rejoice in our pain, even if some around us may seem to feel we can never suffer enough. I have been reminded again and again of Jesus' response when his friend Lazarus died and he was called to come. Even though Christ knew he would later raise Lazarus from the dead to new life, his first response was to weep. I believe he wept in the face of death and loss and in the face of the pain of the remaining family and friends as well.

When I sit and cry and wonder what happened to my sweet little world, when I miss Phil so much that it physically hurts, I no longer feel a punishment from God. I know he weeps with me and for me. I know this because this is what love does and I know that, first of all, God is love.

I am perhaps in a bit of an in-between space in my life. I have heard this liminal space referred to as a "wilderness" for some. A place of becoming, of learning, of coming face-to-face with oneself.

You long for certainty and clear direction, but instead you need the time, this space, to dig deep, to think, to wonder, to pray and to ponder your questions. I resisted this idea with all my being for so long, but I now see it as a sacred space, a place of new beginnings and new life. I feel God is with me here.

I think that we, as the Christian church, have not done a great job at allowing people to voice their most heartfelt and painful questions. We are afraid of them, don't know how to deal with grief or suffering, or maybe we don't even understand it as a body of believers. As a result we shut people down with easy answers, pithy sayings and quotes of Bible verses that irritate and even shame instead of comfort. We approach grieving people logically, but grief is not logical; it turns us inside out. Grief tears us apart.

Questions about pain and suffering and eternity are to be expected and patiently tolerated, prayed, lived and loved through. A rush to find a quick fix or correction can make the mourner feel shamed and misunderstood.

I've wondered during this time if, in our quest for certainty and in our fear of admitting that some questions are simply unanswerable, we trade a false certainty for true, heartfelt and hard-earned wisdom. I have to believe that self-examination and the deeper examination of life itself is never wasted.

As I've spent time praying and living one step forward at a time, I have begun to feel as if God is shining a flashlight on the path in front of me. I wanted to see the entire picture at first, to see all the way down the road to my final destination. I wanted some reassurance about where I was actually going before I took that first step. Maybe I wanted a guarantee. In the midst of my ever-changing and confusion-filled life, that would have been nice.

You might laugh at that. Life simply doesn't work that way. Instead I move one foot and, as I move even ever so slightly, clarity begins to come, to glimmer along the path. It's as if I am holding a lantern in my hand and with each forward motion, I see the path ahead a little more clearly.

I feel led by God, yet I have missed some of the intimacy and the sense of him speaking to me in a profound way, perhaps as a reassurance of sorts. I wanted to be called again, to know for certain, as I had in the past.

I suppose we all long for reassurance, to know that we are seen and deeply loved. To know that in spite of our pain and suffering and wondering and doubts and fears, that God is still right there, even if we cannot feel that reality.

I don't want to confuse anyone and make it sound like I have turned my back on my faith in God. Nothing could be farther from the truth. I would say that I am having to reexamine a few of my long-held assumptions.

I am learning brand-new things in light of brand-new life experiences. These are life lessons I don't know that I could have learned before experiencing such loss. Just as when we physically enter an unfamiliar vista we see things we have never seen before, so is the experience of grief. Since I am in uncharted territory in my life, it's not surprising that God would have fresh things to reveal to me and teach me.

In the midst of change it is normal to reevaluate our lives.

"We sort on the threshold of change; it's how we gather the courage to eventually walk through the door and out into the new day's light."[3]

That is what this time is for me. A time of sorting. A time of wondering. A new beginning. And a little glimmer of light on the path ahead.

It's all a journey. Perhaps we never arrive at all until we are safely home.

27
Grief as the Great Awakener:
I Am Forever Changed

I was recently asked a question that has made me think. A friend looked at me one day and said thoughtfully, "Jan, what are the lessons grief has taught you?"

At first I was confounded. To be honest I wasn't sure where to start because there are so many life lessons I have learned sitting at the feet of grief. (Okay, okay, so I was lying there sobbing.) There has never been a more humbling experience for me personally than the journey of grief. Grief and sorrow have stripped me, changed me, upended my heart, making me more tender and yet somehow tougher all at the same time.

Some things matter more to me now, and some things that used to be of such concern matter not at all. I have become at home with myself in a way I never thought possible since fighting through the muddy swamp of grief, a place I will always traverse to some degree deep within my heart.

In truth, while grief taught me some of life's greatest lessons, it did something even greater—it changed me. "Catastrophic loss by definition precludes recovery. It will transform us or destroy us, but it will never leave us the same. *There is no going back to the past...*"[1] (emphasis mine)

I suppose the first lesson I have learned, the first change I saw in myself, is one of compassion. I have always considered myself a compassionate person, but since losing Phil and going through many problems before his death, I feel even more deeply for people. I am able to be empathetic to the pain of those around me and feel a burden for the hurting in a whole new way. I no longer have any desire to fix but am content just to be with people, knowing that the greatest gift may be the presence of someone who understands.

Along with this empathy, because of my own mistakes and my experience in seeing how life can unravel all around you, I find myself much less judgmental than before. I don't have time or energy to care so much or have an opinion about someone else's life. Frankly it's none of my business, and I've come to see that my job is to love, not judge.

I know what it's like personally to have been through the wringer. My entire life has been shaken and turned upside down and inside out. I understand now how any of us can fall, find ourselves in difficult positions we never dreamed we would face, be totally and humanly frail and just not know which way is up.

I never before understood addiction to drugs or alcohol to numb pain, but I get it now. I have not experienced it firsthand, but I truly get the temptation to go that route when the pain is so pervasive you cannot function and you long to forget. Or perhaps even to die yourself. So I feel now that my response should be one of kindness, not judgment. For most of us the journey is not straightforward, and there are many detours and learning experiences along the way. God can redeem anything—and any of us—through love.

In the same vein I have learned a newfound appreciation for simple human kindness. I suppose it is something most of us take for granted—a gentle word, a smile as someone passes you on the street, an opened door or the listening ear of a stranger, even patience or help when we do not deserve it, a soft hug or quiet understanding from unexpected places. I don't take it for granted anymore. I appreciate it and notice it in an entirely new way.

There was a time when Phil was first diagnosed when I felt like the entire world hated me. This was not true, of course, but what I heard more often than not were hateful words and judgment, gossip, even threats. People showed up to help, but even then I felt that they did it for him, not for me. I heard time and time again how I was talked about, discussed and found wanting.

No one seemed to consider the great pain I had been through and was continuing to go through. I felt utterly alone. I was in a position few of my friends or even acquaintances had ever experienced, and what I most felt was a lack of empathy.

I remember telling someone who voiced their criticism, "If you feel I need to be punished for any mistakes I have made along the way, please be assured that I have. I have never in my life experienced such pain. So try to keep in mind, I live every day with the reality that I will soon be saying good-bye to my husband forever."

What most people never got a glimpse of were the hours and hours of tears that my husband shed, the deep pain we experienced knowing that we could not reverse this or control it, the physical and mental issues that accompanied every moment of life, the hours I lay in the floor screaming out to God, the despair I felt as I knew I could not give in to this grief because someone had to be the strong one, the one who took care of all that needed to be done, the one who held it together when the world fell apart. And that person was me.

All of this to say that I experienced my share of unkind words and actions. Some would say I may have deserved this. I didn't respond well to all I was faced with. But much of the ugliness was unnecessary—and unhelpful.

I felt so overwhelmed by this anger and hate and pettiness that I began to believe the horrible things others said about me, to totally doubt myself, to even doubt that God could love me—after all, my life was totally falling apart; there had been no miracle for me and my family. What did that mean? If God loved me and that is why I am "blessed," what does it mean when life hurts and is ripped away? Am I cursed?

In the midst of all this pain I experienced quiet kindnesses here and there, more and more as time went by. Some were from friends, of course. Phil's coworkers were also unfailingly kind to me, helpful in so many ways, always treating me with respect and even appreciation.

Yet along the way, a great deal of the kindness I encountered came from strangers. I discovered women and men who had gone through the hell of widowhood themselves, and they reached out to me. They did not have to. We didn't even know one another. But they stretched out a hand and a heart.

I encountered people everywhere who were gracious when I cried my heart out to them unexpectedly—from nurses and doctors to sales clerks who asked how I was doing today and got an honest answer and tears. I began to appreciate people smiling at me or opening the door for me, checking on me or going out of their way to make something easier, as I never had before.

I saw the good in others more quickly—and was able to appreciate it more fully. When someone offered to help, I felt more grateful than before. And I began to be more aware and compassionate myself, I think. I appreciate the power of kindness, an encouraging word or a simple gesture, in ways I was never able to before. While perhaps I expected it before, now I don't take it for granted. I was able to accept kindness with a deep sense of gratitude.

I am more closely acquainted with happiness now. I have made friends with it, and I understand it more than I did before. I took it for granted in my past life. I also let myself be robbed of it more than I should have by minor issues in life. I now understand that I must choose to be happy, and sometimes I must even fight for it.

I have learned that God—and life itself—can have beautiful things in store for me in the days ahead, even in this here and now. This beautiful life may not be what I wanted, what I had in the past, what I envisioned for my future, but it can still be a beautiful gift. I must hold out my hands and accept it.

Grief has also taught me to appreciate life as never before. Perhaps that sounds predictable. But it is true. Not only do I appreciate life more, but this has led to acceptance of myself in new ways. In other words, life is short and what is important is so much more than the surface. So now I still get my gray hair colored, but I no longer fret about the fact that I have it. I am not caught up in my appearance as much anymore, although of course I still want to look my best. I understand in a deep way that I am more—and life is more—than how much I weigh or how young I look.

It seems I have lived a million years in this—and gained that much wisdom in the process. This is more important to me than being wrinkle-free at this point. I see beauty and possibility in aging, and am thankful for each new year of life. I do not dread birthdays; I celebrate them.

Am I perfect? No. I am, however, changed in ways that feel profound to me. I am now able to love and accept myself in ways I was not able to before. I am strong and have shown courage. I am a fighter. I have a gentle and tender heart. I am intelligent and willing to learn.

I am Jan. I am enough.

"It is not therefore true that we become less through the loss—unless we allow the loss to make us less, grinding our soul down until there's nothing left...Loss can also make us more."[2] Sittser, widower and author of *A Grace Disguised* continues, "I did not get over the loss of my loved ones; rather, I absorbed the loss into my life, until it becomes part of who I am. *Sorrow took a permanent residence in my soul and enlarged it.*"[3] (italics mine)

At the end of the day I can put it simply this way: Grief, pain and loss have enlarged me, stretched me, enlightened me, remade me. I hope they have shaped me into a better version of myself.

28
I Went Where My Life Led Me

It has been difficult for me to figure out the road forward in the wake of my husband's death. So many questions filled my mind, like a train running relentlessly through my thoughts. The questions were always there.

A line I read this morning, coupled with a long conversation with my son, stayed on my heart and got me to thinking. Following his wife's death, William Bridges said "I went where my life led…"[1] He used this phrase to to describe his navigation of the path of the neutral zone, that in between, almost wilderness place we often encounter in our grief journeys.

That simple phrase felt like such a profound statement. It's run through my head like a familiar chorus. I've turned it over and over again in my heart.

I went where my life led…

I am sitting here with it today, wondering what to do with this piece of wisdom. Bridges spoke of following his own way, the terrain in front of him as he navigated his grief wilderness. Instead of trying to figure it all out, which is a great tendency of mine, he let it unfold naturally. He cautioned against hurrying, against any sort of urgent desire to wrap things up. Instead his advice seems so counterintuitive, "…center yourself and wait watchfully."[2]

The great unknowing is such a hard place to live, to dwell. I won't lie. It makes me a little crazy. A grief counselor once pointed out that this liminal space is a sacred space in our life, a time for introspection and rethinking. I responded—angrily—that it seemed a bit more like hell to me. I was stuck and clueless, which distressed me to no end.

I know that there are those who would argue that we don't ever really know what life holds, and no one knows this better than me, but at the same time it is comforting to have a plan, to have a home base, for the future to not be so wide open in front of you, with no definition at all.

Looking back, I think my equilibrium was out of balance because, even beyond losing my husband, I experienced so many other changes and losses in a short time—and so many of them brought experiences that ran totally counter to all I had been brought up to believe, all I had believed my entire life. Nothing in my life is like I longed for and worked for—in my family or my career. It had all been ripped away, blowing to the winds, and only I was left standing, alone in so many ways.

It seemed as if the guideposts in my life, the rocks, disintegrated and blew away. There was no feeling of sustenance or support—only this vast nothingness and emptiness. I had to learn to let go and open my heart to a new beginning.

So there I stood, no map in front of me except to follow my heart, to take one step forward, then another, as light was given. That is what I have done.

I have focused on one step at a time. I take a test, I finish a paper, I clean out a closet, I pay the bills, I go on a date, I take care of myself and focus on my own healing and this very moment in the present, not on finding answers for the entirety of my future.

Strangely enough, now that I have opened my hands somewhat and emptied my heart a bit in acceptance and have quit fighting so hard to figure things out and solve it all, I am a lot more peaceful. In time these small steps, these small actions have brought needed clarity.

I don't have any answers really. I can't put it in a nice box and wrap a pretty pink bow around the chaos that my life has become. I do, however, feel more peaceful in trying to accept and let go of the need to explain and reach some sort (any sort!) of conclusion. I am now okay to sit with it in this place of "becoming."

In the end I think our great need to explain the hard questions of life is simply a desire for control. If we can explain it, we can figure out how to avoid it or how to achieve it. We—at all costs—want to avoid the hard work and unpredictable experience of simply becoming. Perhaps that is what is truly holy and sacred about this liminal space in the grief journey, this wilderness experience we may walk through—that it is a time of becoming our truest selves.

Death strips us of someone we deeply loved, but the resulting grief can also strip us of things that we needed to shed. This can allow us to become better if we let it. This in-between space allowed me time and a place to focus on dreaming, wondering, paying attention to myself for once and growing as I wrestled with the very real questions grief brings.

It is a slow, wondrous process, not something that happens overnight, and there is no clear finish line in sight. I'm learning to quit fretting so much and to simply enjoy what is in front of me, to lay aside unrealistic expectations—from myself and certainly from others—and to be thankful for what is true in my life. In this process I've learned to accept myself and my life more as well.

So where is my life leading me? I feel like I now have a vision for the future: possibly attending graduate school and a counseling practice to follow focusing on grief work. But I'm still careful not to get ahead of myself. I'm still focusing on one step at a time. One foot in front of the other, following the terrain of my life, enjoying the beauty of this day. In the midst of this, I am getting to know myself as well.

I am listening to my life, going where it leads me.

29
I Have Loved Again...

Almost two years into my journey as a widow, I happily married the man who had become my new best friend. This is a piece I wrote the morning after our wedding.

* * *

I remember talking to a friend a few years back about an acquaintance who had been widowed and then remarried. She said, "I was so surprised when he got married because I don't think he's over his late wife yet. He still talks about her all the time!"

I don't know why this stuck with me, but it did and I have thought of that conversation—and that assumption of life after being widowed—many times as my relationship with Matt (my chapter two and new husband) has developed and deepened.

I've second-guessed myself many times, wondered if I could be ready for marriage since I still routinely have crying spells over missing Phil. I still grieve over all the losses that one enormous, overarching loss brought to my life. I still have so many unanswerable questions—and no certainty on what my future holds, where I'll be working or what I'll be doing. On and on the questions roll, never stopping, it seems. Everything seems so uncertain. So I've wondered a hundred, no, a thousand times what it looks like to be "ready."

I still don't know. I think the answer is different for everyone.

Here's what I do know. Love—and life—always requires risk. It will always require us to take a leap of faith, and it will always require courage we didn't know we had. I woke up one day after so much wrestling over the "am I ready to get married again?" question and suddenly realized that I am better with Matt than without him. I am happier with him. He makes me laugh, brings me joy, encourages me and—yes, some days—he pushes me when I need it. And amazingly enough he doesn't seem to mind when I cry over Phil or have a bad hour or day and need to take a break from the world. He is perhaps more understanding of my need to grieve than I am. How could I say no to this love?

I also know this amazing truth: My love for Matt has nothing at all to do with my love for my late husband. I still love Phil and I always will. I still miss Phil and I always will. I still hurt over losing him, and I am almost certain I always will.

I believe that my life will always carry two streams—sorrow and joy—and they will run through my heart side by side. I never really knew this was possible. I never knew I could know joy and love while still having a crack in my heart. Amazingly, I am able to love and remember and honor Phil while also loving again here on earth. What a gift I consider this to be.

So to those who have wondered if marrying Matt means I "am over" losing Phil, the answer is no. Absolutely not. But the beautiful part of this love after loss is that now I don't have to walk through it alone. I am thankful to be loved and cared for again. I am blessed beyond words.

Christina Rasmussen wrote the following on the ten-year anniversary of losing her husband: "And for those of you who want to know if I am happy again. Yes, I am very happy, but it is a very different kind of happiness. I had to redefine everything for myself because he was not coming back. My innocence was out the door and my heart was in a million pieces. I had to find a way back to life that did not include the old path."[1]

I have shared previously that stepping back into life has been the most courageous thing I've ever done—and that's about much more than dating and remarriage. The old way is gone. That path is not available to me, no matter how badly I might wish to walk it. I am thankful now to be finding a way back to life. Sometimes that requires a big leap, like jumping into a pool of water off a cliff.

I remember as a child we would camp in the Great Smoky Mountains each summer. Oftentimes we would go to a swimming hole in the river and cool off in the frigid waters of the mountain stream. For years I watched the older kids climb up the face of the rock wall on the opposite bank and jump into the deep water there. I couldn't imagine doing it, but one day, when I was about eleven, my dad said, "Come on, Jan, let's go. You're old enough now."

I climbed up those rocky ledges with my heart in my throat and a pounding in my ears. I was a good swimmer, but still I wasn't sure how I felt about leaping off a cliff into the water below. I remember being terrified, but at some moment I chose to close my eyes, let go of the rock I was clinging to, push off from my place of safety and fly!

Whether that leap of faith has been going back to school, applying for grad school, dating, marriage or simply taking a new chance or having a new adventure, I have determined to base my choices on my hopes and not on my fears.

Whenever I feel the fear about any upcoming step in life, I remember a time Phil spoke to me so clearly. One night I had come home from a Krav Maga class where Matt and I had kicked and punched each other and laughed so hard the entire session. I was getting ready for bed, and I had this thought, *I wonder what Phil would think about this?* And at that moment I heard his voice plain as day in my head saying, *Jan, what are you waiting for?*

It's time to live again.

30
It Still Hurts:
Grief after Remarriage

August 26, 2016. Two years out…

Today, just like so many other mornings, I am curled up on the red couch in my living room in my house in the woods, writing out my thoughts, trying to process all the changes in my life. My view is framed by my dog, Ruby, on one side and the beautiful treed view off the bluff on the other. I've been mulling some things over in my head ever since I married Matt this summer, wondering how to put into words what is on my heart.

You see, I woke up this morning like I do every morning since my wedding day—as both a widow and wife. Both are my reality. I hold both truths close to my heart each day.

Yet I have noticed something curious since I married Matt. Every time I mention feeling sad over Phil—missing him or dreading an approaching anniversary, for instance—people are quick to remind me, "Yes, but now you have Matt." It strikes me as dismissive, as if my grief should be less now. Yet people are right. I do have Matt now, and I'm thankful for that gift. I promise I don't take him for granted.

Here's the thing, though. Having a new love, marrying my new best friend, none of that takes away the grief of losing Phil. I still am terribly sad some days. I continue to have flashbacks of him dying. I miss him. I still carry the sorrow around; it is a permanent part of me. Loving again doesn't take any of that away. Loving again does not negate the loss.

I wish it did, and yet I am glad it doesn't. Yes, there is a part of me that wishes to never again know the hopelessness and sadness of seeing Phil suffer and leave us at such an early age. It's not a good feeling.

In another way, however, I never want to forget the pain of losing him. That sorrow that runs like a deep river through my life now, it is a reminder that I loved deeply. That grief has changed me. I would honestly not wish to go back to the person I was before. I carry Phil in my heart forever, and because he is gone from this life, there will always be a bit of pain associated with that love.

I love Matt so much. I'm thankful for having this new beginning, for having a man that—once again—loves me more than I deserve, in a way that amazes me. I am not alone on this journey, it is true. His love helps soften the sharpest edges of pain and has helped heal some of the hurt of the last few years.

But what is also true is that Matt cannot fully comprehend my grief. And honestly, there are things about the grief journey that are ours alone to bear. No one can help us with that or carry it for us. No one can grieve for us or take it from us. Not even God—it is ours alone to walk through. For all that Matt loves me, he cannot fix my grief anymore than anyone else can. It is simply a part of me now, a path I must walk. It cannot be remedied or removed; I must learn somehow to carry it the best I can. Matt supports me, but he cannot take my pain away.

While I now have the blessing of Matt in my life, our family still lost Phil. He still will not be able to walk our daughter down the aisle or watch football games with our son, or watch a silly TV show with our youngest and laugh or a thousand other things. He will not see me graduate from college or hold any grandchildren we might have. Those losses are not diminished by new love or by a new person. People cannot be replaced.

What is true about remarrying is that I do not feel so alone when I have a bad day. I still have those, but I have a bit of a cushion to fall on now. I am so thankful that I no longer walk on my own. I am grateful that Matt is understanding of my needs. He is patient with so many things he might not fully understand.

It's a little surreal for me today, on the anniversary of the day we said good-bye to Phil for the last time. I am once again a married woman, a wife. I wear one man's ring on my left hand and one on my right, and I hold two men forever in my heart. I am deeply blessed and honored to have been loved by two good men.

I do need you to know this today, though. I need to say it. Even with the love, it still hurts.

31
Chasing Sunsets:
Holy Moments in the Midst of Grief

I have to admit to some sadness as I begin this final chapter. I have written furiously for the last two years. Looking back, I believe it would not be a stretch to say that I have written my way back to a sanity of sorts, a place of some kind of peace and healing.

The words poured out of me many times, feelings and experiences demanding a release onto paper. Most of this book was written in "real time"—that is, as it was happening to me. In this chapter I am looking back, trying my best to close out writing about the hardest time of life.

Therein lies part of the problem. My journey is in no way over. I am not magically done as I pen the last few words in this book. But I wanted to finish on a hopeful note, because, as hellish as this journey is, I still maintain the hope and belief that we can be deeply transformed for the better even through—or perhaps because of—our pain.

One thing that has remained true since the first day we knew Phil was dying is that I have constantly looked for signs of hope. Even after the darkest of nights, eventually I felt the desire to live again and to do so fully. I believed life could still be good, that I still had a future and a purpose somewhere down the road.

And so I chased hope, hope that tomorrow could be beautiful, hope that the light was brighter up ahead, hope that God—and the world around me—could use my pain in some way to benefit others. I never totally gave up hope, although I had moments of great darkness when it was tempting to lie down and give up, nights I even prayed to die.

One thing that I often found myself doing in the weeks following Phil's death was taking time each evening to find the sunset. I would drive to the lake and take a walk right before the sun went down, then sit on a bench and watch as the sun slowly slipped over the mountains, bidding the day adieu, the gold of the sun transforming the sky to a pinkish-purple canopy as it sank below the horizon. Other times I'd cross the mountain to watch it slip between the hills. Those moments felt holy to me, peaceful, serene, like a golden time away stolen from the craziness that had become the reality of my life. In those moments I could breathe again, the weight of grief on my chest easing just a bit.

I felt a similar sense of the divine when I would travel on the river on my paddleboard, hearing my paddle slice through the water, the call of the birds from the trees on the shore, the singing of the frogs as the day ended, the distant zoom of boats on the river. The repetitive motion, the nearness of nature, the physical exercise all centered me. Life felt right once again while I was on the water.

This holy peace has overtaken me many times: walking on the seashore, the sand crunchy underneath my feet, water lapping at my ankles, sitting on my back porch listening to the orchestra of insects in the surrounding woods while watching dusk fall on the mountain, unexpectedly in the midst of writing as a truth settled in my heart, while working in my flower beds and seeing the wonder of a rose, as I sat in quiet stillness on the bluff and even, on occasion, in conversations with total strangers. Almost always I am continually surprised as I encounter the sacred amid the mundane—and agony—of life.

I have learned a heart lesson in the midst of the valley of death. You have to maintain an open heart so life can flow in. We might have to purposefully hunt for the lovely, chase the beauty in life, find the good where we can. It is up to us to feed our own soul, to open our heart heart to the holy view we have in this life. And so I chase beauty; I open my heart to it; I hunger for it. And it has helped healed me.

"Gifts of grace come to all of us. But we must be ready and willing to receive these gifts...I will never recover from my loss and I will never get over missing the ones I lost. But I still cherish life."

I will promise you this: if you don't keep an open heart, you will not find life again. You will remain blind to beauty. Your bitterness will bury you, and you will be unable to see the light, the magic, even the kindness of others. The incredible miracles of this world will elude you. I can say this emphatically, because for a time my heart was not open.

Jerry Sittser shares in his classic work *A Grace Disguised*, written after the loss of his mother, wife and daughter all in one moment, that "…the experience of loss itself does not have to be the defining moment of our lives. Instead, the defining moment can be *our response* to the loss. It is not what happens *to* us that matters as much as what happens *in* us."

He goes on to say, "…though I experienced death, I also experienced life in ways that I never thought possible before—not after the darkness, as we might suppose, but *in* the darkness. I did not go through the pain and come out the other side; instead, I lived in it and found within that pain the grace to survive and eventually grow."[2]

Early in my grief journey I realized I was struggling with anger and bitterness. I felt abandoned and alone, unloved and forgotten by others as I traveled what is such an isolating and solitary journey. I soon came to see that these negative emotions were beginning to control my attitude. I was angry over every little thing. My heart was closing up. It hit me one day that I would have to make a choice: to choose joy, to choose life, to choose to love, to choose how I wanted to respond.

Did I want to be bitter? Did I want to allow death and suffering to steal even more of my life than it already had? Or could I, perhaps, allow my pain and suffering to make me better? Could I allow it to develop a more compassionate heart, to grow a patience and kindness in my life that had been lacking? Soon I came to see that it was up to me to make the choice to refuse to allow my loss to define me, and instead begin to fight forward. As a friend so kindly told me, "This is true warrior work."

I learned that the sweet moment was not some far-off distant dream or some long-lost memory never to be captured again—it was in the every-day now. In the sweetness of a hug from a friend, in the beauty of a sunset, in the feeling of the warm sunshine on my shoulders, in the amazement of stepping into the ocean's waves, in the stillness of the dawn, in the furry love of my dog, in the kindness of a stranger.

I kept hoping for joy one day, and I kept longing for what I had once upon a time. I finally realized there was joy and sweet comfort available today. Now. In the present. And this moment, this present time, was really all I could count on. And if that sounds absurdly simplistic, well, I found my heart drawn to the simple joys in life, to what really mattered amid the noise and clutter.

I had to choose to resolutely gaze at the light, at the beauty, in order to heal some of the heartache. I had to focus on what was still good and right in my world—and this was not an easy task. I had to resolutely face forward on days I longed to run back to a past that no longer existed. I had to become conscious of the beauty of the present moment and choose to be present in it.

The fight forward came inch by inch, perhaps millimeter by millimeter. Grief is a journey, it is a battle even, but it is not the end. There can be joy ahead. There can even be joy now. May you find it as you move back into life step by step. Keep fighting forward.

Part 3:

Resources

Help for Widows and Those Who Grieve

*

Things I Wish I'd Known:
Thoughts for Fellow Widows

Look for the help you need. It is more than okay to ask for help, whether that be from a counselor, a bereavement specialist, a support group or a fellow widow. There is no shame and perhaps great benefit.

Grief—widowhood in particular—is a lonely journey. Grief is one of those things no one can do for you, and everyone grieves differently. However, you are not alone! You are still loved, but going through an experience that is *uniquely yours*. Finding other widows that you can interact with online or reaching out to friends who have gone through this experience may help you at least feel understood. I found this true through books as well, but conversation with other widows has been key for me.

Feel what you feel. Your emotions are neither right or wrong. Grieve deeply—emotions are meant to be felt. Grief has a purpose. It might be seen as our escort from what we want (our old life, having loved one with us) to our new reality. It is messy and hard. But in a strange way it is also our friend. It is necessary to spend some time in the dark in order to process your losses. This doesn't mean you have given up. It means you are human and working through a complex human situation. Your days will be filled with highs and lows, and each needs to be treated with respect and understanding.

Listen to your own heart. You know what is best for you, even if others tell you differently. Do you need to get away? Skip an event? Stay away from certain situations? Pay attention to what your heart is telling you. Others' expectations or judgments don't matter. *Your heart knows what it needs.*

Be gentle with yourself. Be kind to yourself. Lay aside unrealistic expectations. Take care of yourself (and your children if you have them) and, for right now, let that be enough. This is one time in your life that it is okay to simply focus on you. *It is okay to take care of yourself. In fact, it is crucial.*

Don't be alarmed if you don't feel spiritual right now. Some people's faith is really affected by grief—this is natural. Your wrestling may one day bring you to a better place. I believe God is big enough for your questions, your silence, and even your anger. You may feel scattered and full of doubts. It's important to feel what you feel without denial. Be where you are right now without guilt or apology.

Focus on what is good. Grief is a fight for your life and heart. So yes, feel what you feel, but choose each day to find something to give thanks for. Simple is okay. I have done this through journaling, on walks, and at different times a Grateful Jar where I wrote down things on slips of paper and put them in a mason jar. At the end of the year I read back through them.

Your life is not over, although it might feel like it. As much as you may want to curl up and die too, I promise you it is possible to still have joy in your life. Know that your life still has purpose. Life is meant for living.

You will grieve other "secondary losses" as well. The loss of dreams and expectations hits us hard as we consider our future. Some days these "secondary losses" don't feel secondary at all; they feel overwhelming. Accepting the fact that the old life is gone and that I have to build a brand-new life is daunting. *One day at a time…one small step at a time.*

One day you will dream again. Don't be afraid. If you think of even a small thing you'd like to do, try it. Or write it down an ongoing list. Lean in and listen to the whispers of your heart.

Your loss will change you. My prayer has been that I will become better, not bitter.

Grief may feel like you are going crazy, but you aren't. You're just grieving. Hold on.

This is your life and yours alone. And it is your only life. I say that no one else gets a vote. That may sound harsh, but it takes willpower and courage to move forward when others might be telling you how you should or should not be doing it. Especially when they have never experienced your reality. Don't be foolish, but do what works for you.

Resources for Widows

Books:

1) *Experiencing Grief* by H. Normal Wright—A short, easy-to-digest book on the basics of grief. It was the first book I read and it helped me understand what is "normal," if there is such a thing, and what is not. It is simple to read in small sections, which is all I could handle at first.

2) *Healing a Spouse's Grieving Heart: 100 Practical Ideas after Your Husband or Wife Dies* by Dr. Alan Wolfelt—Again, this is a book with bite-sized entries, perfect for early grief. Dr. Wolfelt offers understanding and practical steps for those who have recently found themselves among the ranks of the widowed.

3) *A Grief Observed* by C.S. Lewis—This small book is Lewis's journal of his thoughts and feelings following the death of his wife. It's very honest, which I appreciated. A classic on grief.

4) *Second Firsts* by Christina Rasmussen—This book, more than any other, helped me move from longing for death to choosing life. Written from her own experiences as both a grief counselor and a widow, it's a road map back to embracing life. Perhaps best read a few months post-loss instead of early in the grief journey.

5) *A Grace Disguised* by Jerry Sittser—A thoughtful book written by a man who experienced great loss. It describes his personal journey, but also explores questions we have, struggles, and the hope that can still be ours. One of my favorites.

6) *The Year of Magical Thinking* by Joan Didion—This book is a memoir of her experience in the first year of widowhood. Nominated for a Pulitzer Prize, it is a classic on grief and mourning. I was sad when it was over.

7) *Confessions of a Mediocre Widow* by Catherine Tidd—Tidd explores widowhood with both tears and humor. I cried and laughed with her as she shares her journey from loss to life.

Websites:

1) What's Your Grief—www.whatsyourgrief.com Great articles on understanding many aspects of grief. The authors are therapists who have also experienced deep loss themselves. This is an excellent resource for both a clinical and personal understanding of the grief process. There are opportunities for creative ways to journal and express our grief emotions, which I enjoyed. Classes are offered periodically as well. (Can be followed on Facebook.)

2) Second Firsts— www.secondfirsts.com Christina's blog is wonderful. I would highly suggest you sign up for her e-mails, "Message in a Bottle." These messages greatly encouraged me. (Also can be followed on Facebook.)

3) Modern Widows Club—www.modernwidowsclub.com Carolyn Moor mentors widows around the world. There are a few support groups available through this group—check and see if a chapter is near you! (Also can be followed on Facebook.)

4) One Fit Widow—www.onefitwidow.com Michelle writes from her own experience as a widow, with an emphasis on moving and physical exercise. (Also can be followed on Facebook.)

Facebook Groups:

1) Widows and Widowers - Healing, Support and Encouragement—This is a wonderful place for the widowed to find

support and encouragement. You have to be widowed to join and it offers a safety net of sorts for those working through the messy emotions of grief and beginning again. It is a private group.

2) Modern Widows Private Club Membership—You can go to the Modern Widows Club website and join (well worth the $25 annual fee) and have access to private forums, Facebook groups, etcetera to ask questions and get feedback from fellow widowed sisters and brothers. This is also a private group.

Thoughts for Those Who Care and Want To Help

*

Please Let Me Grieve:
A Note to My Fellow Christians

I've been giving a lot of thought lately to a response that I have observed when someone dies, particularly among my fellow Christians. I will call it the "I'm sorry...but" phrase. Generally we hear things like this from those who come to offer condolences, "I'm sorry for your loss *but* he's in a better place now...*but* God is still good...*but* God is in control...*but* he's not hurting anymore...*but* our loss is heaven's gain...*but* nothing can separate us from the love of God...*but* God has a good plan for your life." And on and on. You get the picture.

Like me, you've probably said one or more of these on several occasions. First of all, we simply do not know what to say when faced with someone at their deepest, darkest moments of grief. Grief is messy, and we can all get awkward and tongue-tied when confronted with it.

Secondly, I feel that we Christians especially often feel the need to "make it better" or "point to God" or "remain positive," to wrap it all up in a nice white box and slap a pink ribbon on it. It makes *us* feel better and perhaps protects us emotionally as we consider our own vulnerability to great heartache and loss. We are uncomfortable with not having anything profound to say, so instead we say something stupid. Ask anyone who has suffered a deep loss if these comments are helpful and they will probably—if they feel able to be honest—give you an emphatic "no!"

This is merely a symptom of a greater, deeper issue, the one in which we tend to deny our own—and others'—humanity. Instead of admitting the true nitty-gritty of our grief (or addiction or pain or any other messy, uncomfortable stage of life) or acknowledging it in others, we quote Bible verses or pithy sayings. "God has a plan!" "He won't give you more than you can bear." And so on.

Hear me clearly. I know those are well meaning words. But this is not the most appropriate response. When we try to pretty up the grim reality of people who have lost a spouse or a child or a best friend, when we try to make their loss more palatable, when we deny the terrible mess that death leaves behind, then we deny the griever an important opportunity: the opportunity to be real and authentic, fully sorrowful and, perhaps most of all, simply human.

All the wonderful things we say to try to negate the perfectly awful truth of death are not comforting. In fact, they may make those that are grieving feel alone, unable to express or even admit how they are really feeling. The Bible advises us to "…weep with those that weep" (English Standard Version, Rom. 12:15).[1]

One the loneliest things for me when Phil was dying was that there weren't many people who could be with me, with us, in the reality of our sorrow and grief. We faced the reality that Phil was dying. I even had people get angry with me for saying that he was dying. They would remind me of all their friends with stage IV cancer who were healed (this is not comforting, by the way!) or say, "Well, perhaps there will be a miracle" or get frustrated with my "lack of faith."

All I could say was that this was our current reality and we were not only going to grieve at some future date, we were grieving now. This is real. We live with it every second of every day.

I'll admit it was uncomfortable to be around—that constant knowledge that there is no physical healing to come, no happy ending for our family, no hope for a future with Phil. We were preparing for death, for a new life unlike any we had ever known before—Phil was preparing for eternity, we were preparing to live here on earth without him—emotionally, physically, financially, in every way. That in itself was terribly lonely and isolating for me.

I remember one of the most liberating and profound things that a friend said to me when Phil was hurting and dying. She came to see me, and after we had talked, she spit out a curse word and said, "Well this just sucks!" Then she cried with me. She did not offer a Band-aid or try to pretty it up. She did not offer a religious pat answer. She just sat with me in the messiness and reality of my grief—the tears, the anger, the fear. It was such a relief to be able to simply be myself, to feel what I felt without shame or guilt.

I wrote earlier about my friend Matt and shared how he sat with me in my ugliest moments of grief. He did not try to get me to stop crying or say much of anything. He never tried to take away or fix my grief. He was simply present. This is our greatest gift—someone being present with us in our pain.

When someone is grieving—and we grieve many losses in our lives, not just the physical deaths of people we love—it is important for them to feel seen, heard, and validated. Grief is a lonely, messy place. Without support it can feel too difficult to bear. I have noticed a pattern. When someone experiences a tragic loss and they only talk about the positives publicly, they are praised and held up as an example. "Look at her faith!" or "See how strong she is!" we say, when a woman exclaims on losing her spouse, "God is still good!"

When we repeat this pattern often enough, we send the message that this is all that it is okay for us to say, to acknowledge, to express. We, without meaning to, send the message that the hard things we feel, the questions we have about our faith are better left unsaid. We may inadvertently make people feel guilty for their grief and sorrow, or any seemingly negative emotion—as if their faith is lacking, or they are not a good Christian or a strong person.

How sad and lonely and tragic that is. God never asked us to deny how we feel, to look away from the reality of our lives or to pretend. In fact, Jesus was called "...a man of sorrows and acquainted with grief" (English Standard Version, Isaiah 53:3).[2] The truth is that some things cannot be prettied up. There is no good *"but"* to add to this loss. Some things cannot be fixed or remedied, they are simply our reality and we must learn to carry them the best we can.

A hard truth many of us have learned is that you have to fully walk through grief in order to move forward. You can't deny it, control it, or bypass it. Grief does a necessary work in our lives in helping us adjust to a future we did not ask for or envision. When we deny it, we actually short-circuit our healing. It is healthy to mourn.

I have felt every possible emotion in the past three and a half years. I have been able to stand and praise God, and I have also angrily questioned his sovereignty and love for me. I have run the gamut of emotions, sometimes all within the same hour. I have felt profound sadness and also burgeoning hope and I have had moments of anger and even relief that Phil's suffering was over. I have felt a desire to move forward and also a deep need to hole up in my room and just stay there. I've felt confusion and fear, hope and love, and everything in between. And I firmly believe that is not only okay, it is, in fact, human to do so.

Yes, as Christians we are believers, but we are also human beings and in that humanity, we are fashioned in the image of God. God, as the Creator of us all, is able to handle any of our questions. He can love us even as we question our faith and wrestle with our wonderings and fears. He can bring us hope in the midst of terrible darkness, but he doesn't ask us to deny the difficulty of the journey. I'd say he is honored in our honesty. Let's support one another in that.

So You Want To Help?

Many times I have had friends share with me that they don't know how to help. Widowhood is a loss like no other—it impacts all the nooks and crannies of our lives and leaves so many layers of loss that it may take a widowed person a long time to come face-to-face with all the losses they are grieving. I understand not knowing what to say in the face of the tragedy of losing a loved one. I don't always feel my words are adequate or helpful either. Many times when a new widow shares her story, I just want to cry and I am terrified any words that I might offer will be hurtful instead of helpful.

Nevertheless I think there are some universal truths that might help others be sensitive to what a widow needs. It is always good to seek to be informed and to grow. I learn some new bit of wisdom almost every day about how to respond to people in loss, and I myself have experienced it personally. Grief is messy and unique, and while none of us has a concrete answer about exactly how to respond, we can offer a few suggestions. These offerings came from many discussions with my fellow widows.

It's best not to offer trite sayings that minimize my grief. These don't help; in fact, they hurt me deeply. Instead offer a genuine hug and a simple "I'm so sorry." I'm going to say this plainly: If I am honest, every time someone gives a trite spiritual answer, I want to scream. This minimizes my very real loss, so please, just don't.

Your presence is a beautiful gift. You don't have to say a thing. Just be with me.

Don't say "Call me if you need anything." First of all, I hardly know what I need. Secondly, this puts the burden on me to call you, and I can't handle that at this time. Instead offer a concrete course of help. "Would Tuesday be a good day for me to bring a meal? Mow the grass? Come help with laundry?"

Don't fall away after the funeral. If you said you'd be there for me, please do what you said. Like so many others, I had offers of help while my husband was sick and dying. People surrounded us and worked on the house, brought meals, etcetera. After his funeral, nothing. I felt like I had disappeared, fallen into some hole. No one helped around the house; no one brought food, I felt abandoned. Although I know it is not true, this made me feel as if people loved Phil but not me. Even if it's just a text to say, "Thinking of you today" or checking in with me to see if I am still alive, it helps. Call me just to chat. I may not always feel able to talk, but it will let me know someone cares. Over and over again widows have shared, "I wish people had been there like they said they would be."

Invite me to dinner, to social occasions, to family events. Even if I say "no" ten times, keep on asking. Some days I cannot handle much social interaction, and some days I really need to get out of my house and my own thoughts. Persevere even when I protest. Don't give up on me; include me. So many widows say they feel like a leper now in their own family and circle of friends. Help me begin again by inviting me into your life.

Help me out around the house and yard. By far, when asked what they most needed help with, this is what widows I surveyed answered. Having to become totally responsible for everything pertaining to their home is a new thing for many. Most cannot afford to hire someone, even if they could find help. Simple repairs and upkeep feel monumentally hard when you are adjusting and grieving. A helping hand goes a long way. One widow even shared how helpful it would have been to have someone come teach her about the appliances, circuit breakers, lawn equipment, cars. It's not that we don't want to do it all, it's that we might not know how and it is overwhelming trying to figure it out in the midst of grief. Additionally, it is humiliating to have to ask for help, especially when you ask and no one comes. Believe me, most widows I know won't ask again. But they will still need help.

Respect my need for solitude. Even though I know I need time out and with others, I also know I need time to process my grief and loss and to figure out my new reality. I need time to just cry and be. If I ask for quiet time alone, don't be alarmed. This is normal and needful. Please don't quit inviting me or calling me, but respect that need for space at times. I'm not crazy; I'm just grieving.

Don't tell me how I should be grieving. Or not grieving. Never, ever say to me, "It's been ___ amount of time; you should be getting over it by now!" Don't tell me what I need to do or not do. This grief journey is the hardest thing I have ever done in my life, and I have to listen to my own heart, meet my own needs, take my own time, even reach my own conclusions. I know you want to fix it or make my grief go away. But no one can do that; I will carry this loss forever.

Listen to me! Allow me to share my heart, my feelings. I need friends now more than ever before. I know you cannot understand, but just listen.

If I have children, show them love and don't forget them. Check on them as well, not just me. If I am now a single parent of young children, please help me out so I can have some sanity breaks. Be aware of all I am having to handle, all alone. Being the only parent is frightening and heavy.

Don't judge. Compassion and kindness are what we need. You may not understand decisions I make or how I now react to certain situations, but I am living in a painful place. I am doing the best I can and coping in the healthiest ways I know how. You do not have to agree with what I do or how I live during this time. But I do ask for your kindness. For compassion. For understanding. Negativity? Judgment? Please keep it to yourself.

Be patient with me and try to show understanding. I know my grief is uncomfortable. I know it is hard to be with me right now and my emotions are all over the place. I appreciate your love so much; please be patient. This is a long, messy process, and I need your love and friendship to get through it.

Understand I am changed. The death of a spouse or close loved one changes your perspective. When you live with the reality of dying, you don't give a flying leap about a lot of things that seemed so important just a short time ago. I will never be the same. Please do not expect me to be. My world—and my heart—has been forever altered.

Don't be afraid to mention my loved one. Sometimes it seems people are afraid to mention him because they think it will upset me. On the contrary, I love to hear his name and to reminisce about him. I really enjoy hearing funny and loving stories!

Pray for us and let us know that you love us. Cards, texts, messages—all positive communication helps us remember that in the midst of the darkest days we are loved and cared for. We may not be able to reply, but please believe that it touches our heart.

A Blessing for Those That Grieve

As you grieve your loss—

I wish you a gentle peace in place of turmoil, an acceptance where anger once dwelt.

May you see the beauty that is blossoming in the soil of your own soul—your deep strength, your hard-earned wisdom, that tender frailty, sweet compassion.

May you choose to be kind to yourself as you walk toward healing.

May you sense the reality of the love from others that surrounds you, whether they are physically with you or not.

I wish you the gift of company on this journey that seems so solitary—a hand to hold, an ear to listen, a shoulder to cry on.

May you gain strength and hope from the fellow warriors that walk beside you and before you.

May you have the gift of memories that are sweetened with time to the comfort of an old, soft quilt, stitched with love.

May you have courage and strength for each new day, hour, minute…to face all the newness of life after loss.

May you dream new dreams for a new moment in life.

I wish you the sweetness of seeing the good in life even though you are experiencing so much pain.

I wish you life…sunsets and beauty that stun your soul, friends that bring you laughter, hugs that heal your loneliness.

May you grow better…bigger…stronger…deeper…instead of sinking into bitterness.

I wish you the ability, even on the most difficult days, to run, walk, stumble, crawl toward life.

And may your heartache and loss enable you to reach out a hand of hope and compassion to others along your way.

I wish you sweet peace. And love.

I wish you hope for a new tomorrow that is good.

—Jan Owen
December 2015

Acknowledgments

Thank you. How could I end this book without saying thank you to so many beautiful people? In this journey, the hands that have reached out to pull me up along the rocky mountainside of grief are so numerous. I am thankful for each word of encouragement, each kindness and act of love. I am thankful for those who applauded me as I began to live again. I am humbled by all those who read my many posts on Facebook and encouraged me to continue to write, who saw that perhaps there was something valuable and helpful there to be shared. I am thankful for all the widows and widowers who—out of their own experience of pain—extended a hand to me in my time and offered me the hope that life could once again be worth living. Thank you to my family and friends, who rose to the occasion, loving me in new ways, always supporting my efforts to fight forward.

Thank you:

—*To my widowed friends* who form an unending chain of support—thank you for reaching out to me in love.
—*To my family, including my Mom and Dad,* who lifted me up and carried me, cheering me on and believing in me. I love you so much. You are precious and dear to me.
—*To my children.* May you read these pages—or not—and understand how much I loved your father and how strong I longed to be for your sake. I love you.
—*To my Chapter Two, Matt.* You not only gave me the space to write, but the constant encouragement to do so. Most of all, you believed in what I had to say and its importance to others. I love you dearly. You are my best friend.

—To all those who have gone before me on the journey and whose words encouraged and inspired me daily, authors too numerous to mention. I am forever grateful. These warriors were courageous enough to share their own experiences and resulting wisdom, and I am better for it.

—To my editor and beloved friend, Lea Ann. Thank you for believing in me and using your own gifts to help make this dream come true!

This book is dedicated my fellow widows and widowers, my fellow warriors, with a special shout out to the Good Guys and my friends at Widows and Widowers - HSE, who have shared so much with me. Your stories of loss break my heart while pushing me forward in my desire to equip and empower widows on this journey. Your strength, fortitude and ability to start over and build a brand-new life inspires me daily. Thank you for your support and compassion.

And, of course, this book is finally dedicated to the memory of my precious husband Phil. In life and in death, you touched so many lives, most particularly mine. I will love and miss you forever.

Notes

Introduction to Widowhood

1.   De Santis, M. "These Are the Statistics: Statistics for the Widowed". *Widows Hope,* www.widowshope.org/first-steps/these-are-the-statistics/. Accessed 30 September, 2016.

2.   De Santis, M. "These Are the Statistics: Statistics for the Widowed". *Widows Hope,* www.widowshope.org/first-steps/these-are-the-statistics/. Accessed 30 September, 2016.

3.   "Widow Statistics." *Widows Bridge,* www.widowsbridge.com/stats.asp. Accessed 27 September, 2016.

4.   Sevak, P. "Perspectives: The Economic Consequences of a Husband's Death: Evidence from the HRS and AHEAD." *Social Security Administration,* www.ssa.gov/policy/docs/ssb/v65n3/v65n3p31.html. Accessed 25 September, 2016.

5.   Harma, Risto F. for The Loomba Foundation. *World Widows Report: a critical issue for the Sustainable Development Goals.* 1st ed. London: Standard: Information, 2016. Print. (18)

6.   Harma, Risto F. for The Loomba Foundation. *World Widows Report: a critical issue for the Sustainable Development Goals.* 1st ed. London: Standard: Information, 2016. Print. (18)

Part I: This Is My Story

1.   Commonly attributed to Ernest Hemingway.

Chapter 4: I Think I Might Be Crazy

1. Didion, Joan. *The Year of Magical Thinking.* A.A. Knopf, 2005. Print. (188)

Chapter 7: Spreading My Wings

1.   Unknown.

Chapter 13: How Can I Be Kind to Myself

1. The Bible. English Standard Version, Crossway Bibles, 2007.

Chapter 14: Defending My Grief
1. Bridges, William. *The Way of Transition*. DeCapo Press. 2001. Print. (69)

Chapter 15: It Takes Courage To Keep Living
1. Dickens, Charles. *Great Expectations*. New York: Bantam Books. 1986. Print.

Chapter 16: One Year In
1.   Geffen, David. "The Prayer of Hannah". *Jerusalem Post*, http://www.jpost.com/Jewish-World/Jewish-Features/The-prayer-of-Hannah. Accessed 3 June, 2015.

Chapter 20: I Became My Own Hero
1. Strayed, Cheryl. *Wild: From Lost to Found on the Pacific Crest Trail*. New York: Alfred A. Knopf, 2012. Print.

Chapter 25: Choosing To Live
1.   Geffen, David. "The Prayer of Hannah". *Jerusalem Post*, http://www.jpost.com/Jewish-World/Jewish-Features/The-prayer-of-Hannah. Accessed 3 June, 2015.

Chapter 26: A Different Kind of Faith
1.   Bessey, Sarah. *Out of Sorts: Making Peace with an Evolving Faith*. New York: Howard Books. 2015. Print. (1)
2.   Matthew 27:46. The Bible. English Standard Version, Crossway Bibles, 2007.
3.   Bessey, Sarah. *Out of Sorts: Making Peace with an Evolving Faith*. New York: Howard Books. 2015. Print. (14)

Chapter 27: Grief as the Great Awakener: I Am Forever Changed
1.   Sittser, Jerry. *A Grace Disguised: How the Soul Grows Through Loss*. Grand Rapids: Zondervan. 2004. Print. (73)
2.   Sittser, Jerry. *A Grace Disguised: How the Soul Grows Through Loss*. Grand Rapids: Zondervan. 2004. Print. (49)
3.   Sittser, Jerry. *A Grace Disguised: How the Soul Grows Through Loss*. Grand Rapids: Zondervan. 2004. Print. (45,46)

Chapter 28: I Went Where My Life Led Me
1.   Bridges, William. *The Way of Transition*. DeCapo Press. 2001. Print. (175)
2.   Bridges, William. *The Way of Transition*. DeCapo Press. 2001. Print. (175)

Chapter 29: I Have Loved Again
1. Rasmussen, Christina. "Part Human, Part Something Else." *Message in a Bottle*. 22 July 2016. Web.

Chapter 31: Chasing Sunsets: Holy Moments in the Midst of Grief
1. Sittser, Jerry. *A Grace Disguised: How the Soul Grows Through Loss*. Grand Rapids: Zondervan. 2004. Print. (79)
2. Sittser, Jerry. *A Grace Disguised: How the Soul Grows Through Loss*. Grand Rapids: Zondervan. 2004. Print. (79)

Part III: Resources
1. The Bible. English Standard Version, Crossway Bibles, 2007.
2. The Bible. English Standard Version, Crossway Bibles, 2007.

About the Author

As a "widow warrior," Jan Owen is learning to fight forward and build a new life following the death of her husband of thirty years. As a minister, she uses her heart for others and passion for writing to encourage her fellow widows and others struggling with grief. A new wife and longtime mother, she calls north Alabama home.

Connect with Jan at:

Jan's Website (www.janjowen.com)
Facebook (www.facebook.com/jan.owen)
Fighting Forward FB Page
(www.facebook.com/fightingforwardthebook/)
Instagram (janowen)
Twitter (@janjowen)

Made in the USA
Columbia, SC
13 December 2018